## Our Debt to Greece and Rome

EDITORS

GEORGE DEPUE HADZSITS, PH.D.

*University of Pennsylvania*

DAVID MOORE ROBINSON, PH.D., LL.D.

*The Johns Hopkins University*

# ANCIENT AND MODERN ROME

### BY
## SENATORE RODOLFO LANCIANI
*D.C.L. Oxford, LL.D. Harvard*

## MARSHALL JONES COMPANY
### BOSTON · MASSACHUSETTS

THE PLIMPTON PRESS · NORWOOD · MASSACHUSETTS
PRINTED IN THE UNITED STATES OF AMERICA

# PREFACE

WHEN speaking or writing about Greece and Rome, we are apt to be carried away by the fascination of names and places and depict to ourselves an ideal country, or an ideal city, governed by ideal institutions and inhabited by ideal citizens. We are ready to admit nothing short of perfection when the question concerns the physical and moral development of both Greeks and Romans!

Such a conception has no foundation in truth. The institutions were indeed excellent, but the men were not different from us physically and morally, except perhaps as regards the athletic training of the body. As a matter of fact there was the same struggle for life, the same craving for amusements and the same political unrest; the same habit of depending upon the Government for food and clothing; and, strange to say, the same percentage in the number of publicans as compared with the total population.

When we walk through the streets of Pompeii and Ostia, it requires but a little effort of imagination to recall them to life and make them awake from their sleep of centuries. The pavement we tread upon is the same as that trodden by the Pompeiians and Ostians of ancient times; the water with which we quench our thirst is brought from the same mountain springs; their temples are still open for the worship of the Gods, having in many cases only changed denomination. We can still enter the attractive shops haunted by the fair ladies of the past, where perfumers and jewellers sold their wares, as, in Rome, choosing the Vicus Tuscus for their headquarters; the places where booksellers and copyists (*Librarii* and *Antiquarii*) traded in the Argiletum, money changers and money lenders in the street of Janus, pearl merchants in the Sacra Via, and druggists in the *horrea Piperataria*.

We have inherited from Greece and Rome everything that helps us to fight and win the battles of life, necessities as well as luxuries. We cross the Alps, the Apennines, the Pyrenees, the Balkans by the same passes they first opened through rock and ice, while advancing to the conquest of the world; we harbour our fleets in the same havens they founded in the deep sea; we seek health and rest at the same thermal establishments, which still give fame and prosperity to British, Gallic, German, Helvetian and Italian watering places.

Such being the case, such being the burden of gratitude which we feel, or ought to feel, towards Greece and Rome, I believe that a closer and more detailed comparison between ancient and modern municipal life and management, between ancient and modern Rome, is a subject well worth taking into consideration; at all events, it is a subject less exhausted than, for example, the usual comparisons between Greek, Roman and Renaissance Art. The Romans never boasted of overwhelming skill in painting and sculpture, but they were incomparable architects and engineers. In the following pages, let us consider the magnitude of the debt of gratitude which our modern city owes to ancient Rome in the matter of municipal development, as well as in all the necessities and niceties of life in general. In almost all important matters ancient Rome established a certain standard or type and the reader of the following pages will probably repeat to himself the well-worn but always true adage: *nihil sub sole novum*.

# CONTENTS

# ANCIENT AND MODERN ROME

# ANCIENT AND MODERN ROME

## I. THE SITE OF ROME AND MALARIA

THE Romans did not deny the unhealthiness of the district in the midst of which their Palatine city was built. Cicero calls it a " pestilential region " and Pliny likewise calls the Maremma " heavy and pestilential." Livy, however, says that the Hills were comparatively free from the scourge: a statement, true enough for a certain period, because, towards the end of the Republic and the beginning of the Empire, Rome and the Campagna, hills as well as dales, had been made comparatively free from malaria. Horace's well-known lines

Nunc licet Esquiliis habitare salubribus atque
Aggere in aprico spatiari, quo modo tristes
Albis informem spectabant ossibus agrum

must be taken with caution; of the three temples of the goddess Fever known to have ex-

[ 3 ]

isted in Rome, one stood on the Palatine, one on the Quirinal near the church of S. Bernardo, and a third precisely on the Esquiline near the modern church of S. Eusebio. These three shrines, however, represented the memory of past miseries rather than a contemporary appeal for mercy against the insidious, and very often fatal contagion.

The earliest hints about intermittent ague are to be found in Plautus' *Curculio* [1]: " did the fever leave you yesterday or the day before?" and in Terence's *Hecyra* [2]: " ' What is thy case? ' ' Fever.' ' Quotidian? ' ' So they say.' " Cato distinctly mentions as symptoms of the ague " a black bile and a turbid liver." Pliny says that the excitement of a successful battle, fought on the banks of the Isère in 21 B.C., freed the victorious general from the ' quartan ' fever. " But the nearest approach to the modern theory of infection, through the microbes of ague, is to be found in Varro's *De Re Rustica*, where he contends that in marshy districts ' insects prosper so infinitesimal in size that no human eye can detect their presence.' " [3]

Many attempts at sanitation were made in a desultory way before the Augustan Era, such as the draining of bogs and marshes; the substitution of spring water for that of polluted wells; the sanitary equipment of human dwellings, even when intended for labourers and farm hands; the invention of *columbaria* as places of burial; the substitution of cremation for interment; and lastly, the organization of medical help. I remember seeing a peasant house being laid bare in the farm of Bernardo Lugari, a little beyond the mausoleum of Metella on the Appian Way, and I remember expressing the wish that it should be taken as a model for such structures in our own lands, to-day, so neat were the arrangements of a double floor against dampness; of walls equipped for the circulation of hot air; and other provisions for indispensable accommodations in the house. The results of these sanitary measures were astonishing. Pliny says that Laurentum was more delightful in summer than in winter — while in modern times the place is acknowledged to be one of the most dangerous on the coast. Antoninus Pius and M. Aurelius preferred their villa at Lorium (La Bottaccia, near Castel di Guido) to all other imperial suburban residences; and the dating and address of Marcus' correspondence with Fronto proves his presence there in mid-summer. The same can be said of Hadrian's villa below Tivoli, of the Villa Quintiliorum on the Appian Way, of that of Lucius Verus at Acqua Traversa on the via Claudia, etc. The Campagna must have looked in those happy days like a great park, studded with villages, farms, cottages, lordly residences, temples, fountains and tombs. Whenever a human habitation was to be constructed, the area where it was to be erected was first honey-combed with *cuniculi,* so as to make it free from the least suspicion of dampness. And, as re-gards funeral crypts and *hypogaea,* it is enough to examine the works done around the " Painted Tombs of the via Latina " to dis-cover what care was taken to make them ab-solutely dry.

I can cite personal experience to prove that the present generation has once more con-quered the evil. I remember how, as a young-ster, I used to spend many days in the convent of S. Eusebio, where each of the inmates was asked to take large doses of quinine every morning and evening, so near were we to a hot-bed of malaria. Since then I have spent many, many years of my life in the thick of the once infested districts; for instance at Ostia, without developing the least symptom of disease. Rome has become the best watered and one of the healthiest capitals of Europe, London, perhaps, excepted. We have surrounded it with a belt of absolute security; and even near the former lagoons of Ostia, Ardea, Fregenae, Porto and Campo Salino, cases of malaria have diminished in number and in virulence. Ostia, the population of which, from the beginning of July to the end of September, was formerly reduced to three fever-stricken caretakers, has now become a pleasant rendezvous for Sunday excursionists. Our excellent overseer of the Ostia excavations, Giuseppe Finelli (whose name ought to be mentioned by all lovers of antiquity only with respect and affection) has been living on the spot for many years, winter and summer alike, in absolutely perfect health. Wire nettings against the insidious anopheles have done more for the peasants of the Maremma than the assumption by the government of the preparation and sale of quinine.

## II. WATER–SUPPLY

ONE of the praises bestowed by Cicero on the founder of Rome is: locum delegit fontibus abundantem, "he selected a district very rich in springs." This statement is accurate, as we have descriptions of twenty-three springs within the walls, some of which are still flowing, while others, described by Sextus Julius Frontinus [4] — the well-known Commissioner of Aqueducts under Trajan — have disappeared, owing to the accumulation of the modern soil. Three were held in special veneration on account of their medical efficiency: the spring of the *Camenae* (Muses), just outside the Porta Capena; that of Apollo at the foot of the Palatine, near the west end of the Circus Maximus, and identified with a spring still in existence; and that of Juturna, at the foot of the Palatine, near the house of the Vestals. Frontinus states that for the space of 441 years, the Romans were satisfied with such water as they could draw from the Tiber, from wells, and from some

of the above-mentioned springs. Typhoid
fever must have been rampant until 312 B.C.,
when the first aqueduct was constructed
by Appius Claudius " the blind," who collected
certain springs near the sixth milestone on
the via Collatina. His work may hardly be
called an improvement upon the existing state
of things, for the Appian water was slightly
soapy and warm and unpleasant to the taste.
At all events, once the first step was taken in
the right direction, it was easy to eliminate
deficiencies and to reach perfection. And perfection was reached under the imperial rule
when Rome was endowed with at least fourteen aqueducts, the channels of which reached
an aggregate length of about 509 kilometres
(ca. 315 miles) and discharged *per diem* one
million, seven hundred and forty-eight cubic
metres of water. To appreciate the volume of
such an amount of water, it is sufficient to
compare it with the output of the Tiber, which
discharges only one million, three hundred
thousand cubic metres per day.

If we suppose that the inhabitants of Rome
numbered, suburbs included, one million, there
was a daily water supply, per person, of 1,800
litres. Modern Rome, with a population of

700,000, has about 700 litres per person, de-
rived from four aqueducts: the Vergine (Agrippa's *Virgo*), the Felice (ancient *Alexandrina*),
the Paola (ancient *Traiana*), and the Marcia-
Pia (ancient *Claudia*).[5]

The Vergine springs are located near the
eighth milestone of the via Collatina, in a farm-
house not far from the present railroad station of Salone. Canalized by Agrippa, this
purest of Roman waters reached the city on
June 9th, 19 B.C. The channel was 12 miles
long and the volume discharged in twenty-
four hours, 158,203 cubic metres.

The Alexandrina springs were collected 226
A.D. by Alexander Severus for the use of his
newly built *thermae* in the region of the Campus Martius. The aqueduct, about 14 miles
long, increased the daily water supply of the
city by 21,632 cubic metres.

The Traiana came from various springs near
Vicarello on the Lago Bracciano. It reached
Rome in 109 A.D. The aqueduct, broken, and
repaired many times by the Popes, underwent
a thorough restoration under Paul V, in 1611;
hence the names of Acqua *Paola* and of
Fontana *Paolina,* given in substitution for the
classic denomination. Paul V, however, hav-

ing mixed the good springs of Trajan with the polluted waters of the lake made them un-drinkable.

The Marcia, first brought to Rome about 140 B.C. by Quintus Marcius Rex, has its springs at the foot of the Monte della Prugna, in the territory of Arsoli. Agrippa restored the aqueduct in 33 B.C. Augustus doubled the volume of the water in 5 B.C. Other restorations took place under Titus, Septimius Severus, Caracalla, Diocletian, Arcadius, and Honorius. A very prosperous Company brought it back to Rome fifty-four years ago after an interruption of thirteen centuries, and the inauguration of its terminal fountain on September 14, 1870, was the last public act performed by Pius IX before losing his temporal power.

Connected with the water supply and general welfare of a big city, and essential to its sanitation is the question of sewers. The first attempt towards the establishment of a rational system of drainage was made by Tarquinius Priscus and his host of Etruscan hydraulic engineers. At least, so tradition says. Their prodigious work is still in existence, and still answers in a certain measure its purpose. I refer especially to the Cloaca Maxima, which Livy calls *receptaculum omnium purgamentorum urbis* ("tout à l'égout!"), built twenty-six centuries ago, across a marshy and peaty soil, under difficulties which even in our days would not be easy to overcome. And yet, this Cloaca hardly deserves the title of *Maxima*, because those of the Coliseum and of the Circus Flaminius are its superiors in size, in length, and in the extent of surface drained. I remember the day I entered these subterranean channels, the first time, with a good supply of torches and disinfectants as safeguards against pitfalls and typhoid fever. It was not pleasant, but was exceedingly interesting to follow the stream towards its outlet into the Tiber; in fact, I have known a city engineer, Pietro Narducci, who has spent two or three years of his life in the venerable mire of the Cloaca Maxima and of its side channels. The results of his labours have been made known to archaeologists and topographers in his famous illustrated report.[6]

The drainage system of ancient cities, Rome included, was obviously wrong from several points of view. First, the outlets were used to carry off the sewage and refuse of the town, and, at the same time, the rain water. Secondly, this double employment made it necessary to have large openings along the streets, so that the population was constantly brought into contact with the poisonous gases of the sewers.[7] This state of things has lasted until my own age; and, when I recall the "chiavicone dell'Olmo," from the huge mouths of which myriads of rats used to sally forth at night-time, and when I recall the polluted atmosphere of our kitchens and bathrooms, I wonder of what material our constitutions were made to stand such a state of things without dire consequences. The best apology for it is to be found in the fact that many other European capitals, not to speak of provincial towns and villages, have remained, until recently, in an absolutely identical state.

At the time of Constantine there were in Rome 11 great *thermae*, 926 public baths, 1,212 public fountains, 247 reservoirs, ornamental basins, like the *stagnum Agrippae*, and numerous swimming ponds, without mentioning private houses, public and private gardens, docks and warehouses, each well provided with water.

The *thermae* of Caracalla alone could accommodate at least sixteen hundred bathers at one time, and those of Diocletian double that number. Supposing the average number of clients and patrons for the eleven great *thermae* to have been one thousand, and those of the public bathing houses to have been fifty, we come to the astounding conclusion that 57,000 citizens could refresh and strengthen their bodies in cold, tepid, and warm baths at any hour of the day or night. I have mentioned the night expressly, because we possess the evidence that under profligate emperors these State establishments were kept open until late at night, and even mixed bathing was allowed.

Some of the fountains were of monumental character and rich in works of art. Agrippa, while aedile, decorated those existing at the time with three hundred marble and bronze statues and four hundred columns. We know of one work of art only, an *effigies Hydrae*, which he placed on the Servilian fountain. The fountains of Prometheus, of the Shepherds, of Orpheus, of Ganymede, of the four Fish (*quattuor Scari*), of the three Masks, etc., must have been so named from the statues and reliefs with which they were decorated.

One only of the great fountains has escaped destruction, that popularly called *i Trofei*

*di Mario,* in the Piazza Vittorio Emmanuele
on the Esquiline. The original name of this
clumsy, ungraceful structure is not known for
certain, but I believe it to have been " Lacus
Orphei." The trophies which adorned it were
removed to the balustrade of the Piazza del
Campidoglio at the time of Sixtus V. There
is no doubt, however, that modern Rome sur-
passes the ancient city in the magnificence of
its chief fountains. There are three of them:
the Fontana del Mosé near Diocletian's Baths;
the Fontana Paolina on the Janiculum, and
the Fontana di Trevi near the Corso. The first
was built by Sixtus V with marbles and figures
of crouching lions removed from the temple
of Isis; the second, by Paul V with the spoils
of the temple of Minerva in the Forum Tran-
sitorium; the last, the world-famous Fontana
di Trevi, is immune from reproach, having
been built by Pope Clement XII and by his
architect Nicola Salvi from purely modern
materials. Its water, as pure as the Virgin
who first led Agrippa to its springs, falls into
a basin, as magnificent a piece of work as ever
human genius and skill have created. None
like it was seen in ancient Rome. " Over a
central precipice," to quote Hawthorne's

[ 15 ]

words, " the water falls in a semicircular cascade: and from a hundred crevices, on all sides, snowy jets gush up, and streams spout out of the mouth and nostrils of marble monsters, and fall in glistening drops while other rivulets that have run wild, come leaping from one rude step to another over stones that are mossy, shining and green with sedge."

I wish to add, here, a reference to the *Naumachiae,* on account of the following passage of Frontinus: " I cannot conceive," he says, " why such a wise prince as Augustus was, should have brought to Rome such discreditable and unwholesome water as the Alsietina, unless it was for the use of the *Naumachia.*" This was an artificial lake, oval in shape, 1,800 Roman feet long, 1,200 feet wide, excavated by Augustus in a district of the Trastevere called *Codeta* or *Campus Codetanus,* where sham naval fights were performed on given occasions. But whether the *Naumachia* was a permanent, stone encircled, spectacular place which may have subsisted for centuries, or a temporary, artificial pond which may have had only an ephemeral existence, I am not prepared to state. One thing is certain: that no worse gift could have been made

to the already ill-famed, malaria-stricken Trastevere, because of the fever germs to which the
Alsietina water gave rise; but the *Naumachia*
lay in a quarter of the city where prisoners of
war were relegated, who were placed there,
perhaps, in the secret hope that they would
become the victims of the anopheles.

## III.  HOSPITALS  AND  MEDICAL SERVICE

WE have already made the statement that Rome was an unhealthy
city, but the assertions of Cicero
and Pliny to the effect that it had been
founded on a pestilential site *in regione pesti-
lenti salubris,* must be accepted with caution;
similarly we take with reservation another
statement that the seven hills were " *saluber-
rimi,*" in as much as each of them had an altar
or shrine raised to the " Goddess of Fever."
However, towards the end of the fourth century B.C. the fight against the evil began in
earnest, with the reform of the water supply of
the city, inaugurated by Appius Claudius the
Blind, of which reform I have spoken in the
preceding chapter.  Then came the reform with
reference to public cemeteries, hotbeds of pes-
tilence, which had made many parts of the city
unfit for human habitation.  It is hard to conceive the idea of a Roman *carnarium,* an
assemblage of pits into which men and beasts,

bodies and carcasses, and any kind of unmen-
tionable refuse were thrown in disorder. Imagine what must have been the condition of
these dreadful districts in times of plague, when
the pits (*puticuli*) were kept open by night and
by day. And when the pits became filled, up
to the mouth, the moat which skirted the wall
of Servius Tullius, between the Colline and the
Esquiline gates, was filled with corpses, thrown
in as if they were carrion, until the level of
the adjacent streets was reached. The city
magistrates allowed the daily refuse of a
population numbering about eight hundred
thousand people to be heaped up within and
around the precincts of this Esquiline cemetery. Decree upon decree was issued at a
later age to stop the deadly habit, and a line
of stone *cippi* was set up round the edge of
the pestilential district with the injunction to
keep it free from pollution. No appreciable
results were obtained. My personal experience
in this field of exploration has been exhaustive.
I have found (or I have been present at the
finding of) about seventy-five *puticuli*, grave-
pits or vaults, twelve feet square, thirty deep,
filled with a uniform mass of black, viscid,
unctuous matter, in which only a few bones

could be singled out and identified. I have found a section of the moat of Servius Tullius, one hundred and sixty feet long, one hundred wide, and thirty deep filled with a mass of human remains. Giving to each corpse an average space of thirteen cubic feet, six thousand four hundred bodies must have been thrown into that section of the ditch. I have also found three copies of Police regulations engraved on square blocks of stone, worded as follows: " C. Sextius, Praetor, has set up this line of terminal stones to mark the limits of the ground which must be kept free from filth, carcasses, and corpses." I remember that on the day of the finding of the third cippus, June 25, 1884, I was obliged to relieve my gang of workmen from time to time, because the stench from that putrid ground, turned up after a lapse of twenty centuries, was unbearable, even for men inured to every kind of hardship, as were my excavators.

An account of the successful reform of this matter of cemeterial policy, accomplished by Maecenas, the prime minister of Augustus, and, more particularly, of the substitution of cremation for inhumation is given in my *Ancient Rome*.[8] In the present chapter I shall more particularly deal with hospitals and with the organization of medical service, both civil and military.

Valetudinaria, νοσοκομ ἱα, *infirmaries* rather than hospitals, and other institutions of this kind (in the modern sense of the word), were not commonly known in Rome much before the third century of the Christian Era. In fact, Celsus Aurelianus, an eminent physician of the beginning of the third century, who wrote a treatise on acute and chronic diseases, reproaches the members of the profession for their obstinacy in keeping their patients in absolute confinement. Such a state of things is easily explained. Large houses of well-to-do citizens were each provided with a detached apartment for the reception of sick slaves and freedmen, to prevent the spreading of infection to other members of the household; but there is no evidence of the existence of *public* infirmaries or hospitals in Greece, Rome and Italy until the influence of Christianity began to be felt. Slaves and freedmen, who would have constituted the clientele of the public Nosocomia were, as I have said, well cared for at home at the expense of their masters.[9] The earliest mention of a hospital occurs in Jerome,[10] where we are told that Fabiola, in 360 A.D., gave up a villa, in which sick indigents, lying abandoned in the streets, could be well taken care of. State physicians, who treated the poor gratuitously, in return for their state salary, were provided not only with medicines and surgical appliances, but also with a room or with a suite of rooms called ἰατρεῖα, a term applied also to the consulting or surgical room and dispensary of any doctor. In such rooms patients were allowed to remain for a time, for instance, after an operation, after a confinement and during the early days of their convalescence.

The functions of hospitals for the poor were assumed, to some extent, by the temples of Aesculapius, where the priests, no doubt, combined a certain amount of medical knowledge with a great deal of quackery and superstitious observances. Still there is no doubt that the chief places of study for medical pupils were the Asklepia, where the votive tablets put up by the patients who had escaped with their lives, illustrated a variety of cases, and where new patients were admitted every day. The practice followed by the priests, when dealing with patients of the lower classes, was to shelter them under the peristyle of the temple, *e.g.*, on the island of the Tiber,[11] and to put them to sleep by means of narcotic drugs, in order that in their dreams the gods might suggest a prescription. Once the recipe obtained, the priests themselves undertook the cure; and if the cure succeeded, by some unforeseen and marvellous coincidence, an *ex-voto* was suspended to a nail in the sacristy of the sanctuary, with a tablet describing the happy event. For this purpose there were shops at the entrance of the Fabrician Bridge (now *Ponte Quattro Capi*), leading from the cistiberine city to the Island of Aesculapius, where ready-made *ex-votos* of every description could be purchased. One of these shops was discovered in the Spring of 1885, in sinking the foundations of the left embankment-wall of the river. It contained a quantity of anatomical specimens in painted terracotta: heads, ears, eyes, breasts, arms, hands, knees, intestines, legs, feet, genital organs, etc., beautifully modelled from nature. There were also three life-size human trunks cut open from neck to abdomen and showing the whole anatomical apparatus of the various organs, such as the lungs, liver, and heart.

[ 23 ]

It seems that when there was no more room left for credulous patients within the sanctuary, the sick were exposed in the streets and under open porticoes, in order that passers-by might give them advice from personal experience.

*Medici-chirurgi.* At an early stage in the history of sanitary organization, families of the middle or upper classes were each provided with one or more slaves skilled in medicine, not as a science, but as an empiric practice. Their salary was fixed at 60 *solidi* in gold pieces. The first Greek practitioner, Archagatus by name, arrived in Rome from the Peloponnesus in 209 B.C., but he did not gain much in the estimation of the public. Even in the time of Pliny there were few Roman-born adepts of the healing art, but many trustworthy slaves acted as house physicians. There were recipes in book form, describing the best means to be adopted in ordinary cases. Thus Cato had a formula, of which he made use in dealing with his son, his servants, and his slaves. Aelian mentions a law of the Locrians prescribing that if any sick person dared to drink wine, contrary to the orders of his physician, he was to be punished with death in case of recovery. Members of the profession made up their prescriptions themselves, and either sat in their consulting rooms or dispensaries, or went on a round of visits followed by their attendants, apprentices or pupils. The Asclepiadae were strict in investigating the character and behavior of their students, who were bound by the famous Hippocratic oath — the most ancient medical document in existence.[12]

In their funeral inscriptions,[13] Roman doctors give interesting particulars about their careers. Doctor No. 9572 (*i.e.*, this number is the number of the inscription in the *Corpus Inscriptionum Latinarum*) was attached to the *Ludus Matutinus*, a training school for athletes and gladiators; doctor No. 9585, to the *Praedia Luciliana*, farmlands of the Lucilian family; doctor No. 8907, to the " personnel " of the imperial Libraries; doctor No. 9566 styles himself, *scriba Medicorum*, secretary, I suppose, of a medical association which held regular meetings in a *schola* or hall where its archives were kept. Compare also the funeral tablet of a M. Livius Celsus, *tabularius scholae medicorum*, under the presidency of M. Livius Eutychus, *Archiater*.[14] Mention also occurs of dentists, pedicures, and especially of *medici*

*auricularii,* or ear doctors, and *medici ocularii,*
or eye doctors, like the M. Latinius who practised at Bologna, or the P. Decimius, *medicus
clinicus chirurgus ocularius,* who may have
practised in Rome.[15] They used to carry about
prescriptions for the various cases of bad eye-
sight, engraved in four lines on a carnelian.
Other similar prescriptions concern mostly the
treatment of *aspritudines* (inflammations), *lip-
pitudines* (beady eyes), *caligines* (cataracts?),
*suppurationes* (suppurations), etc.[16]

The profession of dentistry at a very early
date is implied in a remarkable quotation from
the XII Tables; this appears in Cicero,[17]
and relates to teeth filled with gold; we have,
besides, perfect specimens of "bridge work"
in Etruscan skulls, dating from the sixth or
seventh century B.C.

The medical profession was highly remuner-
ative. Democedes began his career at Aegina
at a salary of about 1,550 dollars; followed it
at Athens for a grant of 2,100; and finally set-
tled at Samos, 2,200 dollars having been
offered to him by Polycrates. Cleombrotus
is said to have received one hundred talents
(100,000 dollars) for restoring to health King
Antiochus. We are told of a Stertinius who

[ 26 ]

secured 25,000 dollars a year from private practice, and of a surgeon named Alcon who amassed a fortune of nearly 500,000 dollars in a few years' practice in Gaul.

*Medicae.* Women were attended by *medicae*, or female doctors, such as the Julia Pia, the Minnia, the Torentia, and the Venuleia mentioned in the *Corpus of Latin Inscriptions*. They acted especially as obstetricians or midwives.

*Court Physicians.* Very curious information about the health of imperial personages and their retinue of courtiers is to be found on the gravestones of court physicians. We learn for instance that Augustus was attended by a Caius Stertinius, and, at a later age, by Antonius Musa, a specialist for neurasthenia; this he treated by hydropathy at the Aquae Albulae. Antonius Musa, the most celebrated physician at Rome about the beginning of the Christian Era, brother of Euphorbus, physician to King Juba, became a medical adviser to the Emperor Augustus when the latter became seriously ill. In 23 B.C., Antonius Musa restored him to health by means of cold shower baths and cooling drinks, for which services he was granted by the Senate a large sum of money,

[27]

permission to wear a gold ring as the insignia of knighthood, and a statue erected in his honour near that of Aesculapius. Horace alludes to this cold cure and hydropathic treatment in *Epist.*, I. 15. This treatment, however, failed when applied to M. Marcellus, who died under Musa's care a few months after the recovery of his uncle, in 23 B.C. Musa wrote several pharmaceutical works, frequently quoted by Galen, of which only a few fragments remain. Drusilla, Augustus' second wife, was attended by Hyginus and Cyrus; Antonia, wife of Drusus the Elder, by Epitynchanus. We learn that Tiberius, who was suffering from some kind of ophthalmia, was cured by Thyrius, a *medicus ocularius;* that Hadrian, who was suffering from ear trouble, was cured by Aelius Amyntas, *medicus auricularius,* and so forth.

Coming to more recent years, the office of pontifical *Archiater,* or head doctor to the Pope, was the post most desired by the members of the profession, especially in the Jewish section of the Brotherhood. In fact, one of the reasons for the peaceful life the Jews were allowed to enjoy in the capital of the Christian world, must be found in their skill in medicine, and in their kindness in treating the poor. Towards the end of the fourteenth century a doctor named Emmanuel, and his son Angelo, gained such fame that the City Council, on May 8, 1385, granted special privileges in their favour, " because they are so brave and merciful in the practice of the healing art, attending the needy, gratuitously." These privileges were confirmed in July, 1392, by Boniface IX, in a letter which begins with these words: " Boniface to his dear son, Angelo, son of Emmanuel the Jew, born a Jew, physician and our own companion and guest — ' blessings.' " Martin V and Eugene IV were attended in their ailments by the Jewish doctor Elihu; Innocent VII by Elihu Sabbati, and Pius II by Moses from Rieti. The Aesculapius, the Galen, the Prince of the Jewish medical school in papal Rome was without doubt the Rabbi Samuel Sarfati, who was made *archiater* of the Vatican at the time of Julius II. His wonderful career has been described by Marini in that excellent and exhaustive work, *Degli Archiatri pontificii.*[18]

*Medicinae.* Slaves emancipated after long successful service as doctors in private families, used to end their careers as druggists, apothe-

[ 29 ]

caries and surgeons, performing slight opera-
tions. We possess some notion of their phar-
macopeia. Lucian describes one of these quack
doctors as hawking his cough mixture through
the streets, and promising immediate relief to
all sufferers. In Rome these drug-sellers were
very numerous and flourished so much that
Pliny complains of the want of a law dealing
severely with this breed of impostors. Regular
medicines were sold under the Empire, with a
label specifying the nature and name of the
drug, and of its inventor, the illness it was destined to cure, the component parts, and the
method of taking it.

*Military and Naval Service.* I have found
among the funeral tablets of Concordia Sagit-
taria, the great frontier fortress on the Piave,
one in memory of a Flavius Aristus *Archiater.*
Such a title, hardly known in imperial times,
became fashionable, at least in Rome, in the
fourth century, and it is a strange coincidence
that of four gravestones of such *protomedici,*
three should have been found in the pavement
of the nave of St. Paul's. I am not sure
whether Flavius Aristus was *protomedicus* of
the Garrison of Concordia or of the Municipal-
ity itself. We know that physicians, having

been granted by Augustus exemption from the income tax, had increased in number to such an extent that Antoninus Pius was compelled to limit their number to five in the minor cities, to seven in the larger cities, and to ten in the capitals of each Province. So far as the Army was concerned, each legion was granted from one to three *medici ordinarii,* a title which makes us think that in war time *extraordinarii* may have been called into service. There are also records of a Tiberius Julianus, *clinicus* of the fourth battalion of Praetorians; of a Bononius, *medicus castrensis* at Lyons; of a M. Ulpius, *medicus* of a squadron of Indian auxiliary cavalry. There were also doctors for the Praetorian and Urban *Cohortes,* for the Police and Fire Departments, for the *Equites singulares,* etc. So far as the Navy is concerned, it seems that each man-of-war had on board its own physician, at a double salary, as shown by the epitaph of a M. Satrius from Baiae, who calls himself *medicus duplicarius* of the three-decked war vessel, " Cupid."

Mention is also made in military epitaphs of surgeons or *chirurgi,* especially qualified for the treatment of wounds. Celsus gives as requisite qualities for this class of practitioners

[ 31 ]

(sometimes called *vulnerum medici* or *vulnerarii*) a steady hand, a keen eye, and middle age. An army doctor ranked among the *principales* or officers. The superintendent of field hospitals was technically called *optio valetudinarii*.

*Hospitals of Later Times.* In later times there is no denying that hospital institutions were brought to a much higher standard, even in the darkest periods of the Middle Ages. The fact is easily explained. Christian charity, good-will, and feelings of Christian Brotherhood had become the moving spirit of their organization, and sick people were no longer considered as an objectionable burden, but were made comfortable and taken care of as if they were members of one family. Hospices for pilgrims multiplied, especially in the neighbourhood of the great basilicas. Wealthy citizens turned their splendid palaces into *valetudinaria*, or built these *ex novo*, like the " domus Valeriorum " on the Caelian; the " domus " or " portico of Galla " near the Forum Boarium; the " domus Pammachii " on the Caelian hill; the " domus Fabiolae " (probably) on the Aventine; the hospice of Belisarius on the Campus Agrippae, each of which became a harbour of refuge for the poor, especially for infirm pilgrims bound for worship at the *limina Apostolorum*. It has been my privilege to discover, excavate and describe one of the richest hospices for transmarine pilgrims landing at Porto. It was in the shape of cloisters, with two wings, or dormitories, capable of holding twenty or thirty beds each, enclosing a beautiful church rich in marble decorations. Tradition attributes its construction to Pammachius, son of Bizantes, the same who transformed his house on the Caelian into a church sacred to the memory of John and Paul, the victims of the persecution of Julian the Apostate. I discovered this beautiful building at Porto in 1868, and its preservation was so marvellous that even the silver spoons and forks and the silver plate were found in their proper places in the pantry or refectory. Prince Alexander Torlonia made a present of this precious *supellex* to Pius IX, but many specimens were stolen by the workmen, and sold to an antiquarian in Naples.

The most important group of hospices or *scholae* in Rome was that surrounding the Basilica of St. Peter. It comprised the *scholae*

[ 33 ]

of the Anglo-Saxons, of the Frisians, of the Franks, and of the Longobards.[19]  Of their national churches, three out of four are still in existence, *viz.*, S. Maria in Saxia, S. Michele dei Frisoni, and S. Salvatore in Terrione dei Franchi.  The fourth dedicated to St. Justin seems to have disappeared at the beginning of the fifteenth century.[20]

The other, smaller but very numerous medical institutions of the city can be studied from the point of view of their special purpose, or of the corporations to which they belonged, or of their nationality.  The first type includes the hospitals of S. Gallicano for skin diseases, of S. Giacomo for " incurables," of the Consolazione for wounds, of the Pietà for nervous disorders, of S. Rocco, a maternity hospital, of S. Trinita for the *pellegrini,* of S. Giovanni for convalescents, of Santo Spirito for foundlings, etc.

The second includes the hospitals of S. Lorenzo for the apothecaries; of St. Elizabeth for bakers, etc.

To the third class belong S. Maria dell' Anima of the Teutons, S. M. di Monserrato of the Spaniards, S. Antonio of the Portuguese, the Flemish S. Giuliano, S. Luigi of the

Franks, the Polish Sudario, S. Claudio of the Burgundians, S. Stefano of the Moors and Abyssinians, besides Italian hospices of the Florentines, Lombards, Bergamasque, Genoese, Sicilians, etc.

The reader may judge of the wealth and splendour of these institutions from one instance only, that of the hospital of Santo Spirito in Sassia, which, in its origins, dates back to the time of King Ina the *Saxon* who about 717 A.D. founded a house of refuge for pilgrims of his nation.[21] Pope Innocent III (1198–1216) tried to restore its fortunes and to prevent its total collapse, but with no tangible results. It was only in the last quarter of the fifteenth century that Pope della Rovere, Sixtus IV, aided by Baccio Pontelli, his favorite architect, built what even now is considered to be a prototype of a State hospital. The hall was 500 feet long, 50 wide, with a portico on the street side, containing a number of fire-places or stoves, for the comfort of the beggars who congregated under its shelter to gather the remnants of the food supplied to the inmates. There are reasons to believe that the altar under the central dome was designed by Andrea Palladio. Should this tradition be true, this altar is the only work of that excellent architect existing in Rome.

The hospital of Santo Spirito was called the richest landowner in Italy. To it belonged the whole stretch of territory crossed by the via Aurelia, between Vaccarese and Civitavecchia, as well as the delta of the Po, including the farmlands and the big game preserves of la Mesola.

## IV. THE PALACE OF THE CAESARS AND THE PALACE OF THE POPES

IN Murray's *Handbook*,[22] the description of the Vatican group begins with the following sentence: " There is no other palace in the world which approaches the Vatican in extent and interest, whether we regard its prominent position in history, or the influence exercised by its collections of art and learning for more than three centuries over the intellectual world. It is an immense pile of buildings, irregular in shape and plan, constructed at different times, without any regard for the harmony and cohesion of the whole."

The same praise and criticism might be applied to the Palace of the Caesars, in the construction of which every Emperor, from Augustus to Septimius Severus (28 B.C. to 211 A.D.), seems to have taken a conspicuous part, without any concern for the general effect. The Palatine Hill, so near the Capitol and the Forum, both, centres of political and business life, had always been the favorite residence of statesmen, lawyers, orators, and wealthy citizens. Here dwelt M. Fulvius Flaccus, whose house was levelled to the ground after his execution for his share in the conspiracy of the Gracchi — and Q. Lutatius Catulus, consul 102 B.C., with Marius, with whom he gained the victory over the Cimbrians near Vercellae — and M. Livius Drusus, the great reformer of social laws, whose murder by Q. Varius was immediately followed by the Social War. His house was inherited by Crassus the Orator, who, having ornamented its *impluvium* with four columns of Hymettian marble, was nicknamed the " Palatine Venus." Cicero bought it in December 62 B.C., for a sum corresponding to $155,000. After passing through other hands it was finally absorbed into Caligula's palace. Mention also must be made of the house of Quintus Cicero, brother of M. Tullius, of Clodius, the notorious foe of the orator, and of M. Aemilius Scaurus, stepson of Sulla the Dictator, which was afterwards purchased by Clodius for an enormous sum.

Augustus, born near the north angle of the hill, in a lane called *ad Capita Bubula* (at the Oxen heads), selected it as the Imperial residence. After the death of Julius Caesar the property was enlarged by the purchase of the houses of Catiline and of Quintus Hortensius, a man of immense wealth, and formed a parallelogram six hundred feet long, four hundred feet wide, comprising the Propylaea, the Temple of Apollo, the Portico of the Danaids, the Greek and Latin libraries, the shrine of Vesta, and the State and private apartments.

Tiberius added the *Domus Tiberiana* and the House of Germanicus; Caligula, a wing called *Domus Gaiana;* Domitian, a palace named *Aedes publicae populi romani,* besides trying to give a certain amount of unity to these independent structures. The one, however, who succeeded in doing this is the good Emperor Septimius Severus, who ruled Rome and the world from 193 to 211 A.D. He actually increased by one-third the area of the imperial residence by raising enormous substructures, from the level of the Circus Maximus to that of the ground floor of the Palace, — a difference in height of 150 feet.

Recent excavations have allowed us to solve many problems, and discover many details concerning the administration and inner life of this small imperial city. But many points are

still enveloped in darkness. For instance, we
know that for the use of the Emperor, of his
family, of his suite, of the officers on duty,
of the guests, there was an army of cooks so
numerous that they had a private hospital, and
one or more attending physicians, *medici coco-
rum*. The state banqueting hall has been
found; other small *triclinia* have also been
found, but not a trace of a kitchen or a
pantry, although it has been suggested that the
well descending to the lowest level of the palace, in which some metal pulleys were discovered, may have been used for a dumbwaiter.
Another point which is still waiting for a
satisfactory explanation is the total absence
of toilets, if we except a diminutive corner,
back of the state banqueting Hall. I may also
mention as a point of comparison between the
imperial and pontifical palaces the fact that
their enclosures were so skilfully arranged that
a handful of men could guard the gates at
night with absolute security for the inmates.
As far as the Palatine is concerned, there were
only three *corps de garde,* one at the Gate of
Victory, the walls of which are covered with
interesting but improper *graffiti;* the second
at the top of the stairs of Cacus; while the

location of the third has not yet been discovered. Such is the case with the Vatican of to-day. Having once closed the bronze doors entrusted to the care of the Swiss Guards, or those of the Belvedere guarded by the Pontifical Gendarmes, the whole Vatican is as secure as if it were not a fictitious but a real prison. Leaving aside the church of St. Peter and its annexes, the pile of buildings connected with the habitation of the Pope contains the state stairway (Scala Regia), the reception hall (Sala Ducale), the Sistine Chapel with Michelangelo's "Last Judgment," the Cappella Paolina built in 1540 by Paul III, the Library, the Picture Gallery with the "Transfiguration" by Raphael, the Loggie painted by Giovanni da Udine, the Gallery of Raphael's tapestries, the Gallery of geographical maps, the pontifical Armoury in which is kept the steel armour of the Connétable de Bourbon, which he wore when killed before the Castle of St. Angelo in 1527; the Garden with its extensive groves of ancient oaks, and the Casino built by Pius IV from the designs of Pirro Ligorio in accordance with the plan of a Roman villa, just discovered on the shores of the lake of Gabii. The Museum itself, the extent of which exceeds several thousand feet and which requires many hours for even rapid examination, contains 15 wings, galleries or halls, the names of which are known over all the world, so as to make full description of them, here, quite unnecessary.

When we consider that the Vatican palace occupies an immense rectangle 1,151 feet long and 767 feet wide, and that the number of its halls, chambers, galleries, etc., almost exceeds belief, we may easily class it among the wonders of the world. According to trustworthy calculations, it contains eight state stairways, two hundred smaller ones, twenty courts, four thousand and twenty-three rooms. If it is further considered that the Sistine Chapel possesses the "Last Judgment" of Michelangelo; the Pauline Chapel, two frescoes by the same master; the big gallery of inscriptions, over two thousand specimens of palaeography; the Braccio Nuovo, the Nile and the Apoxyomenos; the Rotunda, the Mastai Hercules and the Juno from Lanuvium; that the picture Gallery contains the famous "Saint Jerome," the "Transfiguration," the "Madonna" of Foligno; the Library, thousands upon thousands of precious manuscripts; that the Stanze were painted by Raphael, the Loggie by Giovanni da Udine; that the Etruscan Museum contains the *Regolini Galassi* tomb, the richest in existence, we may safely say that in this kind of architectural and ornamental wonders modern Rome has the advantage over the ancient, and that the Pope's residence exceeds in magnificence even the Imperial Palace of long ago.

# V. SHOOTING LODGES OF EMPERORS AND POPES; THE PRESENT ROYAL PRESERVES OF CASTEL PORZIANO (LAVRENTVM); ZOÖLOGICAL GARDENS

ONE of the most striking coincidences in the succession of things from ancient to modern times is to be found in the hunting lodges of Emperors, as inherited by the Popes.

We knew from an inscription discovered at Laurentum that the beautiful pine forests, stretching along the coast from Ostia to Antium and to the promontory of Circe, constituted a domain of the crown, under the management of a head gamekeeper (*Procurator Laurento*). These forests were teeming with wild boar and stags and deer, and have remained so until quite recent times. I have before my eyes a plan of the Roman Campagna, drawn by Innocenzo Mattei at the time of Alexander VII (1655–1667), in which the territory in question is marked with the legend:

" Selve di capri e damoli " (forests of stags
and deer); in fact, when I first began watch-
ing the excavations at Ostia in 1871, I remember meeting many times groups of sportsmen,
carrying homeward the trophies of the day.
Game and forests have, alas, disappeared, and
we owe a debt of gratitude to our good King
for having recalled to life and for having proclaimed as a sanctuary some fifty thousand
acres of game land. A section of this estate
was set apart in imperial times for the breeding of elephants, and when the estate was
inherited by the Popes we know that another
section was given up to the breeding of pea-
cocks (*Paunaria*). The knowledge, however,
that the forests of Castel Porziano were used
in classic times for the same purpose as at
present, and that they were watched by a
body of gamekeepers, similar to those who
wear to-day the King's grey uniform, was obtained only in 1909 by means of an inscription discovered by our gracious Queen, whose
name no Italian can mention without feelings
of devotion and gratitude. The inscription
describes how a certain Aglaus, president of
the guild of imperial gamekeepers (*Collegium
saltuariorum*), had offered to his fellow workers

[ 45 ]

a set of portrait busts of their sovereigns (*imagines dominorum nostrorum*), to be set up either in the meeting room (*schola*) of the guild, or else in the local Augusteum, remains of which are still extant in the forum of Laurentum. It seems that the free life of the woods, and the breathing of air sweetened by the emanations of resin must have made these men long-lived, if we may judge from the ripe age of eighty-five reached by Eutyches, *saltuarius* of a preserve near Nuceria Alfaterna.

At the time of Constantine the property, and, consequently, the right of hunting big game was transferred to the churches of the Saviour in the Lateran and of the Holy Cross (Santa Croce in Gerusalemme). What became of it in the Middle Ages is not known. The forest spread across the viae Ostiensis, Laurentina, and Severiana; the pines and ilexes thrust their roots into the pavement of the roads and into the crumbling walls of the villas which once lined the coast; the sea receded; sand dunes rose where palaces, cottages, villages had stood. The old kingdom of Turnus and the whole *silva Laurentina* were broken up into the farm lands of Fossignano, Porci-

gliano, Buonriposo, Veprosa, and others. Then
came the inroads of the Saracens from Algiers
and the revival of malaria in its most virulent
form. This plague, as already explained, has
now almost disappeared, thanks to the work
of sanitation introduced by our King.

The hunts in the Roman Campagna were
first resumed at the time of Eugenius IV
(1431–1447) by Cardinal Mezzarota Sca-
rampo, a warrior more than a churchman, the
wealthiest man in the country, and a great
breeder of horses and dogs. It is true that the
sacred canons forbade clerics to devote themselves to pastimes of this kind, but in those
happy days such small deviations from the
rules were easily forgiven. Another name de-
serving a place of honour in the annals of sport
is that of Ascanio Sforza, the Nimrod of the
Sacred College, whose memory is still preserved
in Rome in the name of the street (Vicolo d'Ascanio) which led to his kennels and mews
in the Campo Marzio. An eye-witness, Cardinal Adriano Castelli da Corneto, has left a
brilliant description of a hunt given by him
at the *Aquae Albulae* (Sulphur Springs) on
the road to Tivoli, at which meet was present

a " Gueldrian named Libs, the inventor of a fearful engine of destruction, such as not even the Cyclops could have devised for the use of Jupiter. It consists of a tube of metal loaded with sulphur, natron, and ground charcoal, the mixture being sealed on the top with a lead bullet." [23] This man Libs must be considered therefore as the inventor — not of portable firearms in general — but of a light kind of fowlingpiece more adapted for the shooting of big and small game. His name, however, is not mentioned in Dutch or German biographical dictionaries.

The Popes themselves had more than once taken an interest in hunts, but as simple spectators. On the occasion of a meet arranged in honour of Borso d'Este by Pope Paul II, a medal was struck showing a hunting scene, with the motto: *solum in feras pius bellator Pastor* (the pious shepherd wages war only against the wild beasts). Leo X, however, was the first Pope to surround himself with the retinue of men, dogs, horses, and snares necessary to ensure success to real regal sport. He could not follow the hounds on horseback, on account of his corpulency, but sat on a stand from which a good view of the field could be obtained. When the chase came to an end, he would gather his guests for suitable refreshments in the hunting lodge of la Magliana, which stood close by.

A visit to la Magliana on the road to Porto (the ancient *via Campana*) is highly interesting in spite of the vandalism which the lodge has suffered not so much at the hands of time, as at the hands of greedy despoilers. The name is a derivation from the classic " fundus Manlianus," the suburban farm of the Manlian family, known in history since the year 390 B.C. Here a pontifical cottage was founded by Sixtus IV (c. 1471–1484), afterwards enlarged and beautified by Innocent VIII, Julius II and Leo X. The latter held a consistory in one of its halls, while the chase was at its height, but, alas, caught there his last illness in 1521. After Leo's death, Pius IV occasionally resided at la Magliana, his name and coat of arms being sculptured in various parts of the building. Sixtus V is the last Pope mentioned in connection with this suburban residence, which soon after was abandoned to farmers, who quickly destroyed the fine works of art it once contained, save a set of frescoes attributed to Raphael, though more probably of the Perugia

School, which were purchased for the Louvre by President Thiers in 1872.

In the autumn of 1874 another set of frescoes by Lo Spagna, which adorned the consistorial hall, representing Apollo and the Nine Muses, was removed to the Conservatori palace on the Capitol. For many years they had been hidden under a copious whitewash, while the legs and feet of all the beautiful figures were destroyed by the labourers, who had driven or hammered pegs into the wall, on which they might hang their clothes. The situation of la Magliana is enchanting and much has been done by the National Government to free the district from malaria.

Speaking quite broadly, there is a marked difference in the treatment of dumb animals in ancient and modern times. First of all a distinction must be made between the chase of ferocious beasts, to provide victims for the games of the Amphitheatre (*Venationes*) and fresh stock for the Zoölogical Garden, and honest sport in the modern sense of the word.

The capture of ferocious beasts was entrusted to a specially selected body of hunters, who wore a multi-coloured uniform not unlike that worn to-day by the Swiss Guards at the

Vatican. They were trained, according to the needs of the government, to capture the special kind of animals they were expected to gather, such as bears and elks from the Carpathians and the Balkans, elephants from Africa, leopards from Syria, lions from Nubia, tigers from India, amphibians from the Nile, etc. While waiting to be slaughtered in the arena the animals were kept in a Zoölogical Garden or *Vivarium,* adjoining the Praetorian Camp, from which it was divided by a partition wall. The four sides of the square (700 ft. × 800 ft., the last vestiges of which have been obliterated within my recollection) were lined with cages large enough to ensure ample freedom of movement to the beasts, who could drink and bathe in the waters of a channel (*Euripus*) which ran close to the railings. The Roman " zoo " could well stand comparison with the best institutions of the sort of the present day. At the time of Gordianus the Younger, 244 A.D., it contained, besides a vast number of smaller animals, 30 elephants, 10 elks, 10 tigers, 60 tame lions, 10 hyenas, 1 hippopotamus, 1 rhinoceros, 19 giraffes, 20 wild asses, and 10 wild horses. Connected with the *Vivarium* was an Amphitheatre, still in existence, where the

beasts were trained to perform the most incred-
ible exercises, and the hunters were trained
to the various manners of sport. There was
also a special staff of doctors or *veterinarii*,
to watch over the health and hygienic needs
of the beasts.

Dogs were divided into three classes: *canes
villatici*, watch dogs, whose office was to guard
farmhouses against the aggression of thieves;
*canes pastorales* or shepherd dogs for the protection of sheep from robbers and wolves;
*canes venatici* or sporting dogs. They were
provided with iron or leathern collars, spiked
with nails, from which hung labels giving the
name and address of their owner, with the request that, in case of attempt to escape, the
runaway should be arrested and brought back
to his master. Nineteen such labels have
already been found, the legends of which are
worded more or less in this way: "I am the
dog of Felicissimus, head shepherd to the
Basilica of Paul the Apostle," or, "hold me
because I have run away, and take me back
to Leo, the caretaker of the Basilica Aemilia."

Besides the plaster cast of the Pompeian
dog taken by Fiorelli in the house of Orpheus,
of which we have a good reproduction in

Thédenat's *Pompéi*,[24] we actually possess, although in a mummified state, a beautiful sporting dog, a greyhound, three thousand, three hundred years old, discovered by Theodore Davies in the sepulchral chamber of King Amen-hotep II at Biban-el-Moulouk. King Amen-hotep was very fond of pet domestic animals, above all of monkeys, ducks, and chickens. The Egyptians, to speak the truth, seem to have mummified everything that had had life, — animals, birds, fishes, insects. Witness the great cat necropolis at Bubastis, the ibis cemetery at Abydos, and the jackal cemetery at Deir-el-Bahari.

In preserving larger beasts it was not the custom to embalm and mummify the whole body. Thus a sacred cow would be represented by the horned head alone, with a small selection of bones.

The only grave of a large animal, found within my own recollection in the Roman Campagna, is that of a bull, buried in a coffin at the Mezzo Cammino, the half-way house on the road to Ostia. The explanation of such an unusual burial has yet to be found.

# VI.  HOMES

**B**UILDINGS for human habitation in
Rome were of three kinds: private palaces or private houses (*domus*), for the
residence of one patrician family, with a more
or less copious retinue of freedmen and slaves;
apartment-houses in the strictest modern sense
of the word (the existence of which has just
been made known by the latest excavations at
Ostia); and thirdly, tenement houses (*insulae*), many stories high and capable of accommodating many families.  At the time of
its greatest prosperity Rome is said to have
numbered 1,790 *domus* and 46,602 *insulae,* the
population not exceeding eight hundred thousand souls.  These statistics refer only to the
fourteen wards (*regiones*) of Augustus, enclosed, at a later age, within the walls of
Aurelian; but there was a suburban belt of
houses, lodgings, hostelries, with gardens and
orchards between them, extending for a radius
of at least three miles from the Golden Milestone.  All, together, they formed the metro-

politan district, under the care of special magistrates *viis in Urbe purgandis.*

*Insulae,* tenement houses and " skyscrapers," unknown in villages and in provincial towns like Pompeii, Herculaneum, Ostia, and Velleja, were introduced into Rome in 455 B.C. We can get no better evidence of the fatal law which divides men assembled in a city into the few who possess much and the many who possess nothing, than the manner in which the few and the many are housed.

There were hardly 1,800 families of wealth in old Rome, enjoying the luxury of a palace or a private mansion, while many thousands of families were massed in the 46,000 tenement houses hardly fit for human habitation. These were not well built, their foundations were not sunk to the proper depth; their front walls were only a foot and a half thick and patched up with sun-dried bricks. At the time of Vitruvius, about 15 B.C., their construction had undergone some improvement, thanks to the energy of Augustus, and thanks also to the increase in the value of ground, which compelled builders to gain in height what they were losing in surface. Strange to say, the new tenements were constructed on somewhat the same principle that prevails now for American skyscrapers, attaining a considerable height and capable of accommodating as many families as there were floors, perhaps even two families for each floor. But their spontaneous collapse was such a common occurrence that nobody paid attention to it. Cicero speaks of the fall of some cottages attended with loss of life as an item hardly worthy of remark. Seneca depicts the tenants of certain homes, as fearing at the same time that they might be burned or buried alive. Construction companies were formed for the purpose of propping and sustaining " in the air " houses, the foundations of which also had to be strengthened.

Archaeologists have collected the following information as regards house rents in Athens and Rome. In Athens lodging houses were let mostly to foreigners who came to the capital on business. The banker Pasion had one valued at one hundred minae, or two thousand dollars. City property yielding a return somewhat more than eight and a half per cent on the purchase money is mentioned by Isaeus. Boeckh says that rent varied from sixty to a maximum of two thousand four hundred dol-

lars, according to size, location, and comfort of
house. Rents were commonly paid by the
month. Lodgings were frequently hired on
speculation by obscure individuals, who made
a profit by subletting them, sometimes for not
very reputable purposes. In Rome rents were
equally high, even for a miserable garret. Persons in the lowest walks of life paid 2,000
sesterces. Coelius is said to have paid 30,000
sesterces for a third floor in a tenement of
Publius Clodius. Hence it became a profitable
speculation to build or to hire a whole block
and to sublet the single rooms or suites to different tenants, the whole establishment being
placed under the care of a controller called
*Insularius*. Noblemen owning a large town
property counted among their clerks a *procurator insularum*.

We come now to the question of the height
of buildings. The excessive elevation of tenements is noticed for the first time, I believe,
in Cicero, who compares Rome suspended in
mid-air with Capua lying comfortably down in
the plains of Campania Felix. Seneca complains of the impunity which builders of tall
*insulae* were allowed to enjoy, because the poor
tenants, perched in those heights, had no pos-

sible escape from fire or from the collapse of the building itself. There is no doubt that towards the end of the Republic Rome had higher houses than some modern cities. While the building act promulgated in Berlin in 1860 admits a maximum of thirty-six feet only, provided the street is of the same width; while the Viennese act allows forty-five feet, and the Parisian sixty-three and a half, higher figures were tolerated in ancient Rome with no consideration whatever for the width of the street. Augustus, to obviate disaster, limited the height of new houses to seventy feet, at least on the street side, and later emperors made similar provisions.

The house door was watched by an *Ostiarius* or porter, whose duty was to admit visitors and to prevent anything improper from being carried into or out of the house. It was also his duty to sweep the ground-floor rooms. Plato gives a lively picture of an officious porter boring visitors to death. He was generally assisted by a dog. On the threshold the words *Salve* or *Cave Canem* were frequently wrought in mosaic, as we see many times in Pompeian houses; and over the threshold there sometimes hung a cage containing a magpie (*pica saluta-*

*trix*), or a parrot (*psittacus*) to greet those who entered. Over the door a few words of good omen were written, such as *nihil intret mali* or *deprecatio incendiorum*. Sometimes the house was marked by a sign over the door, generally by the image of a god or goddess under whose protection the inmates were supposed to be. We are just discovering at Ostia a beautiful house with the sign of Diana. The town address of resident citizens was specified in the same manner as it is now, namely, by means of the region and by the name of the street. Thus, we are told that Augustus was born *ad Capita Bubula*, Domitian *ad Malum Punicum*, etc. *Insulae* were designated by the name of the owner. Thus we have records of an *Insula Bolaniana, Sertoriana, Vitaliana, Felicles*.

The value of town property was very great indeed. The house of L. Crassus, the orator, on the Palatine, built about 92 B.C., was valued at six million sesterces or about 62,000 pounds; but Pliny says that it yielded in magnificence to the house of Q. Catulus on the same hill, and was much inferior to that of Aquilius on the Viminal. Hymettian marble was first used by Crassus, Numidian by Lepidus in 78 B.C. In spite of the criticisms of the few who were still devoted to Republican simplicity and austerity of life, luxurious and costly dwellings grew so rapidly in favor that hundreds were raised before the Augustan age, Lucullus being specially praised for the beauty of the large garden which surrounded his town residence, and which soon became state property, under the name of *Horti Luculliani*.

The house of Aemilius Scaurus was sold to Clodius for nearly fifteen million sesterces, about 132,000 pounds, a price, as Pliny says, worthy of the madness of kings. It is the highest price recorded in pre-Augustan times. Again, we hear that the Consul Messalla bought his house for 29,000 pounds and that Cicero gave 30,000 for his residence. These examples of the cost of mansions of the nobles may give a fair idea of the value of town property and of the immense size and wealth of these houses. Sallust compares them, in size, to small cities, and Seneca describes them as equal to the imperial palace. In course of time the burden of keeping them up in style became so heavy that they were either sold or given to the State, together with the large gardens by which they were surrounded. This is the origin of the *horti Sallustiani, Luculliani, Lamiani, Variani,* etc. The first of these gardens was laid out by the historian Sallust with the money accumulated during his governorship of Numidia; the second, by Lucullus and Valerius Asiaticus; the third, by Lucius Aelius Lamia, consul 3 A.D.; the fourth, by Sextus Varius Marcellus, father of the Emperor Heliogabalus. I have myself discovered or seen discovered many of these princely residences within or without the walls of the city. I shall never forget the excitement I felt on Christmas Eve of 1884, when a wing of Caligula's cottage in the Lamian gardens was discovered about nightfall. I ran to the spot as fast as my feet could carry me and helped the men dig out, one by one, the most exquisite works of the ancient chisel that have ever been found collected in a single room. I worked like a slave until one o'clock in the morning. We were in a portico, inlaid with about thirty varieties of alabaster, with tiny jets of water leaping from panel to panel, to keep the place cool and the flowers blooming. There were colonnades of fluted shafts of *giallo antico* (Numidian marble), the capitals of which must have been of gilt metal. There

[ 61 ]

was lying on the exquisite floor the bust of
Commodus under the attributes of Hercules,
flanked by two Tritons or marine Centaurs,
and by two statues representing either Danaids
or Muses. There were the lovely "Venus
Lamiana," a portrait head of young Commodus, a head of Diana, a Bacchus of semi-
colossal size, with drapery of gilt bronze
(missing) and about twenty-five exquisite
fragments belonging to statues whose drapery
was likewise of bronze. If we recollect that
from the same mansion and from the same
gardens came the "Meleager of Belvedere,"
the pediment of a temple (?) with the slaughter
of the Niobids, now in Florence; and two
Athletes, also in the Uffizi Gallery; the "Nozze
Aldobrandine" now in the Vatican; the "Dis-
cobolus" of Myron now in the Lancelotti Palace, and hundreds of other celebrated works
of ancient chisels, and a gilt bronze *cathedra*
or *lectica,* studded with precious stones, not to
mention coins, gems, and medals, our mind can
hardly grasp the significance and the importance of such a collection.

Equal in size and beauty, although despoiled
of its artistic treasures, was the Casino or
Villa discovered in the gardens of La Farnesina

in 1884, on the right bank of the Tiber, the paintings and stuccoed panels of which now form the best ornament of the Museo delle Terme. As I have already given a detailed account of this find elsewhere,[25] I shall not attempt any further description, here. " It seems as if Baldassare Peruzzi, Raphael, Giulio Romano, il Sodoma, il Fattore and Gaudenzio Ferrari, to whom we owe the wonders of the Farnesina dei Chigi, must have unconsciously felt the influence of the beauty of the Roman house which was buried under their feet. It is a great pity that the two could not have been left standing together. What a subject for study and comparison these two sets of masterpieces of the Golden ages of Augustus and of Leo X would have offered to the lover of art."

To come back, however, to the more immediate subject of this chapter, which concerns especially private dwellings, I may remark that high pitched roofs, covered with tiles, were not used in Rome, but only in districts subject to snowstorms; otherwise they were generally flat so that the tenants of the upper stories could walk about on them; could, as is done to-day, dry their linen in sunshine (hence called *solaria*); and could even pass from one house to the next in case fire broke out unexpectedly in their flats. In later times these *solaria* on the tops of houses were turned into roof-gardens, which contained even fruit-trees and fish ponds. There were in use also awnings to make the *solaria* agreeable during the hottest hours of the day.

It is incorrect to suppose that *insulae* and *domus* had no windows overlooking the street, when any number of such, — sometimes opening on wooden or stone balconies (*maeniana*), — are actually to be seen at Ostia, and in Rome itself, as, for example, in the house of John and Paul, in the imperial mansion within the Sallustian Gardens, and in the house embedded in the walls of the City on the right of the Porta S. Lorenzo.

The *latrina,* or privy, was as a rule in close and dangerous connection with the sink of the kitchen, so that a common drain might carry off the refuse of both. In palaces, such as the one in Hadrian's villa, and in that of Augustus on the Palatine, the lavatory was a richly and beautifully decorated apartment, with several jets of water and accommodations for six or eight people. Such an extraordinary arrangement has lasted in Italy until my own age. I remember having seen one in a convent near Urbino, with ten seats, such as we have seen provided during the late war for the use of our soldiers at the front. For the above-mentioned house of Diana at Ostia, which was at least three stories high and comprised at least six apartments, there was only one retreat and a very indecent one at that.

Rooms were occasionally heated in various ways: first, by being built in that part of the house which faced the south, hence their name of *Heliocamini;* secondly, by means of charcoal braziers, such as we still find in use in many places, to-day. Fireplaces seem to have been unknown. Hot air from the hypocausts was made to circulate under the floors and even under the plastering of the walls, by means of tiled flues, so that the inmates of the house were never brought in direct contact with the burning embers and with suffocating fumes from the furnace.

These comforts for pleasant living, within the walls of a city house, were extended even to cottages for the farmers of the Campagna. I remember the discovery made not many years ago on the farm of Tor Carbone, belonging to the late Cardinal Lugari, of a rustic dwelling of a modest appearance but wonderfully well adapted to its purpose. Its ground-floor rooms were provided with double pavements or floors for the circulation of hot air, while great care had been taken to carry off the drainage to a great distance by means of a permanent stream of water, part of which was also stored in a reservoir or cistern, ready for any extraordinary emergency.

I cannot prove in a more convincing way the statement that modern Rome compares advantageously with the ancient City, as regards palaces, gardens, and villas, than by citing what one single man, Cardinal Alessandro Farnese, was able to accomplish under the pontificate of his grandfather, Paul the Third. His palace, which constitutes even in our days of luxury and display the most splendid creation of the Renaissance, became the recipient of the rarest and best collections ever formed by a private individual. The collections comprised works of statuary, pictures, books, manuscripts, inscriptions, *objets de vertu,* medals, coins, engraved gems, miniatures, invaluable books and curiosities, exhibited in halls designed by Michelangelo and

by Antonio da SanGallo, and painted by Anni-
bale Caracci. The collection of statuary included many direct products of excavations,
but it was also enriched through purchases.
The Farnese Museum represents to us the sum
of the efforts which had been made, independ-
ently of each other, by Cardinal Marino
Grimani, Bernardino Fabii, by the brothers
Sassi, by Tommaso della Porta and other col-
lectors, to secure for their respective homes the
best specimens of statuary that they could
obtain.[26]

When we think, therefore, that the Farnese
Palace contained at one time such masterpieces
of ancient art as the " Flora," the " Punishment
of Dirce," the " Hercules " of Glycon, the
group of Atraeus, the " two Gladiators," the
so-called " Hermaphrodite " of touchstone, the
" Marcus Aurelius," the " Sabina," hundreds of
minor statues and bas-reliefs, mosaic pictures,
the marble plan of Rome, drawn at the time of
Septimius Severus, the *Fasti triumphales et
Consulares,* and the richest spoils from the
Portico of the Argonauts, from Trajan's Forum,
from the Curia Athletarum, the Roman Forum,
the Regia, the Baths of Caracalla and Diocletian, the Gardens of Caesar, from Bovillae,

Tibur and Tusculum, we can safely maintain that the Farnese Palace at the time of its glory outrivalled any other similar creation of human genius in ancient or modern times.

Before the sack of 1527, Cardinal Alessandro, then residing in the old Ferriz palace, kept a princely court of his own. In the census taken under Clement VII a few months before the dire event — the results of which were made known in 1894 by Domenico Gnoli [27] — Cardinal Farnese ranks next to the Pope and above all his colleagues of the sacred college, as regards the number of his courtiers and servants. To the Pope are assigned seven hundred "bocche," or mouths feeding at his expense; to the Cardinals, the following retinues: Farnese 306, Cesarini 275, Orsini 200, and so on until we reach the more modest suites of Cardinal Numalio with sixty servants, and of Cardinal Vio with forty-five.

# VII. PORTICOES, A CHARACTER-
ISTIC ROMAN INSTITUTION

AN institution very popular in ancient
Rome, but which has not been
adopted by any modern city,[28] is that
of the garden-porticoes, large parallelograms
of green enclosed by a colonnade. At the time
of Rome's greatest prosperity, the surface of
the Campus Martius and of the Circus Flaminius, in fact, the whole area between the
left bank of the Tiber and the Pincian, Quirinal, and Viminal hills, was covered with
porticoes, " greens " and " campi," twenty of
which are especially mentioned by ancient
authors. Under the Republic, when the habits
of the population had not yet been influenced
by enervating contacts with Greece and the
East, the few existing porticoes were devoted
to practical purposes. The *Minucian* served
as a corn exchange, the *Holitorian* as a market
for vegetables, the *Pompeian* to give shelter
to the people sitting in the adjoining theatre
in case of a sudden shower. Augustus made

the institution popular by building a great
many with his own money, or by asking
wealthy friends to follow his example. In the
space of twenty years the whole Campus Martius was covered with colonnades. Augustus
built those of *Octavia,* with the Greek and
Latin libraries; the one called " ad Nationes,"
and a third called *Corinthian* on account of the
gilded bronze capitals of its columns. Then
Cornelius Balbus built his *Crypta* and Philippus the portico surrounding the temple of
Hercules Musarum. Agrippa outstripped his
predecessors and contemporaries in the magnificence and the magnitude of his structures.
To him we owe the *Porticus Vipsania,* the
*Septa Julia,* the *Villa Publica,* the *Portico of
the Argonauts,* and the one of *Europa.* So
popular became the institution that new colonnades were added to those already mentioned,
even until the fall of the Empire and the
subsequent establishment of papal rule, when
it was possible for pilgrims to proceed under
shelter from church to church, and from the
centre of the city to the outlying sanctuaries
of St. Peter, St. Paul and St. Lawrence.[29]
Finally, we have documents concerning other
great structures which had been begun but

were left unfinished by their promoters, as, for
example, the *Basilica* of Severus Alexander,
one thousand feet long, one hundred wide, and
that of Gordianus the Younger, which was to
measure one thousand feet in length and forty-
four thousand square feet in surface. The
same fate befell the *porticus* of Gallienus, a
prince well known for the extravagance of his
artistic conceptions. Among other curiosities
he caused a formidable colossus to be erected
on the top of the Esquiline hill, in the middle
of the Licinian Gardens. It would have measured, when complete, two hundred and thirty
feet, that is to say, three times the height of
the statue of S. Carlo Borromeo at Arona on
Lake Maggiore, and more than twice the height
of Trajan's Column. The figure was adorned
with symbols of the Sun and it held a rod
in its right hand enclosing a spiral staircase,
by means of which a little boy could reach
the summit. Another of his extraordinary
projects contemplated the building of a portico about three thousand yards long between
Rome and the Milvian bridge on the via
Flaminia.

I do not know whether due consideration
has been given to the special nature of these

edifices, stretching along the river from the foot of the Aventine to the region of the Vatican. They have been studied rather individually, one by one, and from this point of view they appear to us sometimes as enclosures of temples, sometimes as art galleries of painting and sculpture, or as a meeting place for the fashionable idle youth. Their importance increases tenfold if we consider them all together as successive manifestations of the same idea, as a part of a single scheme for the benefit of the public. Rome was certainly not lacking in parks and gardens. Both summits and slopes of the chain of hills framing the valley of the Tiber, from the Pincian to the Varian Gardens on the left side, and from the Minucian to the Caesarean on the right side, had been turned into two immense public parks of rare beauty. On the right side of the river the line of public gardens culminated in a Belvedere (now the Villa Aurelia, the incomparable seat of the American Academy), from which point of vantage the eye wandered from the snowclad Apennines to the pineclad coast of the Tyrrhenian Sea. These public parks, however, were naturally exposed to the rigours of the seasons: to the sharp blasts of the

Tramontana in winter, and to the heat waves of the dog days. To better the situation and to give to the people of the metropolis a chance to wander in every season of the year, at every hour of the day, sheltered from rain, and sun, and cold, this system of porticoes was adopted: or rather, it was suggested that buildings, which up to that time had had a different use, should be exclusively set aside for the benefit and pleasure of the public. It is manifest that this happened when the old severe habits of life were modified or corrupted by Eastern ideas. Nature and art were made to harmonize: pleasure was sought as much as usefulness. For instance, on the enclosure wall of the Portico of Vipsania Polla (the sister of Agrippa) the maps of Rome, of the XI Italic Regions, and of the whole Roman world were exhibited; on that of the Argonauts, the fresco paintings represented the tale of the Golden Fleece. The Septa Julia were taken advantage of for the exhibition of curios, antiques, products of the far East, and natural wonders, such as a serpent fifty cubits long, and a beam of larch one hundred feet long and three feet thick and wide, cut from the forests of the upper Adige. Finally, the portico of Philippus

[ 73 ]

was used for the exhibition of wigs and the latest fashions in ladies' head-dress.

Should the reader lay before his eyes a plan of the ancient city,[30] he would see at once how easy and delightful it must have been made for the citizens to walk under shelter from the Forum Boarium (la Bocca della Verità) to Hadrian's mausoleum at the opposite end of the town. And the sight was enough to captivate even the most torpid minds. I have been tempted to calculate some statistical data concerning this incomparable group. The extent of the twelve larger porticoes of the Campus Martius amounted to 4,600 yards; the surface protected from sun and rain, to 28,000 square yards; the total area of the porticoes, central gardens included, was 100,000 square yards; the number of columns, 2,000 or thereabouts. The columns were sent, cut from the rarest kinds of marble; their capitals were of Corinthian gilt brass; the pavements were inlaid with jasper and porphyry; the walls were adorned with statues, bas-reliefs, and pictures, while the inner space was decorated with lovely gardens and clusters of box, myrtle, laurel and plane trees, intercepted with lakes, fountains and waterfalls.

Much has been said about Roman taste in the matter of gardens. It was very poor, or at least it was an exaggeration of that kind of taste displayed again by Renaissance architects and landscape artists in Rome, Florence, and upper or central Italy. Trees were not allowed to grow according to the provisions of nature; they were cruelly pruned and made to look like wild animals and monsters hiding in sylvan recesses. Then, the supply of flowers was very limited. Nevertheless, although the flora of those days was but poor in comparison with ours, there is no proof of the assertion that the Romans contented themselves solely with wild plants, and neither laid out flower gardens nor cultivated any exotics. Violets and roses were certainly the main ornament of pleasure grounds. Next came the bulbous roots — the crocus, narcissus, lilies of many kinds, iris, hyacinths, poppies, amaranthus, and so on. The Roman flower par excellence was the rose. So excessive was the demand for this flower in the cold season that, to supply the requirements of the market and to meet the deficiency of native production, they were imported even from Egypt, Syria, and Phoenicia. The same means were employed to keep them as fresh

[ 75 ]

as possible which we use throughout the winter, who import flowers from the Riviera to our picturesque market on the Spanish Steps. Another place famous for the winter trade in roses was Paestum and the surrounding lowlands, bordering on the Gulf of Salerno. *Biferi rosaria Paesti* Virgil (*Georg.*, iv. 119) calls those gardens, because they bloomed for a second time in the late autumn.

Entire absence of natural beauty and stiffness were, as I have just said, the characteristics of an ornamental Roman garden, in which no tree or shrub dared to grow in its natural form. At all times the gardener was ready to force them into prescribed forms. In the leafy avenues bordered by walls of green box and laurels, with their windows, doors and niches imitating the architecture of palaces, appeared, here and there, threatening forms of wild beasts or snakes winding themselves round the trees, all cut by the skilful hand of the *topiarius* from cypresses, yew trees and myrtle. The reluctant foliage was compelled to simulate letters, spelling in one part the name of the mistress of the domain, and in another the name of the artist to whose invention the garden owed its appearance.

Grounds laid out in this geometrical style, by which every vestige of nature's freedom was annihilated, were not only praised by ancient writers (as by Pliny, as in the case of his Laurentine Villa), but were painted, I might almost say photographed, in the frescoes of Pompeian dining rooms. The same style appeared, doubtless, in the gardens of Maecenas, in those of Aelius Lamia, on the Esquiline, and in those of Livia's Villa on the Flaminian Road. It is evident that foreign countries had not yet revealed to the Romans their inexhaustible variety of shrubs and flowers. The trees represented in the frescoes of the Villa of Livia are the pomegranate, the laurel, the stone pine, and various kinds of firs, arbutus, ilexes, plane trees, myrtles, and cypresses. Restricted, thus, to a barren flora, little improved by culture, the Romans sought to create by artificial means a striking contrast to the free forms of nature.

The garden paths were usually arched over by trellises or by green arbours of canes and vines, and their floors were sprinkled with yellow sand.

Before bringing this chapter to a close, and without entering into more particulars, I

[ 77 ]

must say a few words of my own personal experiences in connection with the discovery of one of these great structures of ancient Rome, so essential to the welfare of the Metropolis, namely the *Portico of the Argonauts*. It was erected by Agrippa in 26 B.C., in commemoration of his naval victories over Sextus Pompeius, for which he had received the naval crown: and also in memory of the share he had taken in the battle and victory of Actium. The group comprised a temple of the God of the seas (a considerable portion of which, including eleven columns of the north side, is still standing); a garden-square 325 feet long, 292 feet wide, enclosed by a colonnade, upon which opened halls of various kinds, mostly occupied by the offices of the Imperial Admiralty. The group was called *Neptunium*, while the portico took the name of the Argonauts from the paintings of naval subjects which it contained. Like the temple of Isis, the Pantheon, the Thermae, the Septa, and the Diribitorium, it came to grief in the great conflagration of 80 A.D., but it was restored by Hadrian.

To appreciate the value of the discoveries which I was able to make in 1876 (acting as

Secretary to the Municipal Archaeological Com-
mittee), it must be remembered that the outer
wall of the basement (or *podium*) of the Temple was decorated with figures, as bas-reliefs,
personifying the thirty-six Provinces of the
Empire, one beneath each of the thirty-six
columns, while the spaces between were ornamented with panoplies. Three figures of
Provinces and two trophies were discovered
under Paul III and removed, first, to the Palazzo Farnese and then to the Museo Nazionale
of Naples, except one fragment left in Rome.
Under Innocent X, two more figures, representing Provinces, were dug up and presented
to the Capitoline Museum. The trophy set in
the wall of the first landing of the stairs of
the Altieri Palace was probably discovered at
the time of the Altieri, Pope Clement X.
Under Alexander VII (Fabio Chigi) another
couple of figures of Provinces was found *in
situ,* under two of the existing columns. The
Pope, as usual, kept them for himself, and they
are still to be seen in the staircase of the
Chigi-Odescalchi Palace in the Piazza dei
Santi Apostoli.

In 1876 I had the chance of bringing to
light six more bas-reliefs in the Piazza di

Pietra, placed upside down in the pavement
of a medieval church, called S. Stefano del
Trullo.   On February 9, 1883, three more
pieces were dug up from the same place, making a total of thirteen Provinces thus represented and of six panels.   If the wishes of
artists and archaeologists had been consulted,
Provinces and Panoplies would have been
restored long ago to their original places, so as
to make the remains of the Temple of Neptune
one of the most beautiful and impressive existing monuments of Ancient Rome.   No admiralty palace of modern Europe could be
compared with the beauty and splendour of
Agrippa's masterpiece.   The request which I
made in the year 1883 for the restoration of the
building was not granted by the State, and the
sculptured panels were allowed to remain
scattered in five palaces or museums, in two
cities two hundred miles apart.

As I have stated above, the example set by
Augustus and his courtiers found imitators
down to the fall of the Empire: witness the
*Porticus Maximae* of Gratian, Valentinian, and
Theodosius, and also the colonnades, or shel-
tered ways, which led from the Aelian Bridge

to St. Peter's, from the Porta Ostiensis to St. Paul's, and from the Porta Tiburtina to St. Lawrence's. I am among the few who have seen remains of these *Porticus Maximae,* which are partly in the foundations of the Santa Croce Palace, partly in the trenches dug for the drainage of the *Via Arenula.* I gave strict attention to the excavations, in the hope of tracing the effects of the earthquake of 425 A.D., which disaster is known to have caused the collapse of the *Porticus Nova.* The indications were scanty, yet I could ascertain a certain amount of parallelism in the downfall of the columns, as if the shock had come from the southwest towards the northeast, — a detail which has also been noticed at Ostia, in the ruins of the so-called Imperial Palace, in the church of Santa Petronilla on the Via Ardeatina, and in other places. I may remark, also, that, as in classic times triumphal arches were raised on the Sacra Via leading to the Temple of Jupiter, so in the Christian Era, arches were raised on the roads converging towards St. Peter's; and especially at the approach of the bridge which the pilgrims were bound to cross on their way to the Apostle's tomb. That of Theodosius, which stood at

the entrance to the Aelian Bridge (Ponte Sant'
Angelo), bore an inscription stating that it
had been raised *ad concludendum opus omne
Porticuum Maximarum*.  Other particulars
about this late network of green spaces and
colonnades are to be found in the Guidebooks
and Itineraries for pilgrims, the earliest and
best of its class being the one formerly in the
library of the Abbey of Pfaeffers, later in that
of St. Mary of Einsiedeln.  I have published
this venerable document (in fac-simile) to
prove that in the ninth century, at the time
of Charlemagne, the preservation of the sheltered highways from Basilica to Basilica was,[31]
if not perfect, at least certainly excellent.

## VIII. LIBRARIES

THE oldest written document which has come down to us from the earliest times of Rome, namely the *stele* of the Forum,[32] proves how uncouth the language, how crude the spelling, how incorrect the manner of writing of our remote ancestors was. They used in fact the *boustrophedon* system of engraving their records, so called because the lettering begins from right to left and goes on alternately from left to right, like the tracing of a furrow in a wheatfield. And as our progenitors were men of action rather than men of letters, and more prone to use the sword than the pen, it is evident that public and private libraries must have been instituted at a very late period. The first important one, mentioned by Varro, had been brought over by L. Aemilius Paulus, the conqueror of Macedonia, from the palace of King Perseus, among the spoils of war. Sulla the Dictator, when in Athens, laid hands on a far richer collection, namely, the library of Apellikon, which had belonged previously to

Aristotle himself. Pomponius Atticus, the faithful and intimate friend of Cicero, seems to have formed his library more for love of money than for love of literature. He was the confidential agent of Cicero, not only in the search for new books or new editions, but as an organizer of the temples of learning. His two assistants, Dionysius and Menophilus, had so skilfully put in order Cicero's library, that the illustrious orator could not help writing a letter of thanks to his friend Atticus, the bookseller. Strange to say, even at this early stage of bibliophily there were men who stole books. One of Cicero's trustworthy servants had run away with a certain number of volumes, and had been followed by detectives to the coast of Dalmatia. "The theft was materially of no importance," said Cicero, "still I feel the loss very much."

I shall not follow the development of these institutions, or mention the names of Roman benefactors, in whose footsteps modern patrons have stepped, such as the popes, Sixtus IV and Sixtus V, for the Vatican library, Cardinal Neri-Corsini for the Corsiniana, Cardinals Chigi, Barberini, Casanate for those bearing their names.

In 1752 a private library was discovered at Herculaneum, with shelves lining the walls of the apartment, and one bookcase standing by itself in the middle of the floor. Altogether there was room for 1,700 volumes; rather too many from our point of view, i.e., for one chamber; but then we must remember that ancient libraries were, probably, never warmed, even in the depth of winter, in order to avoid dangers of conflagration and the inroads of moths. Hence the necessity for making use of small rooms and of overcrowding them with shelves. That is the reason why we, ancient students of the Vatican Library, perished with cold, for four or five months of the year, until Monsignore Achille Ratti, then librarian to the Holy See, and now welcomed to the chair of St. Peter's by the whole world with joy and satisfaction, caused the reading room to be comfortably warmed.

The great book market, the Paternoster Row of Ancient Rome, was the Argiletum, a quarter situated between the Forum and the Subura. Here the *librarii* and the *antiquarii*, booksellers and copyists, kept their well-furnished stores, so often mentioned and described by Horace and Martial. On each side of the

entrance door were hung elaborate advertise-
ments, giving the title and the price of literary
novelties, and even the portrait of the author.
As regards public libraries, our knowledge of
their organization has been made more complete by the discovery, made by Albert Ballu,
of the municipal library of Timgad. We have
learned for the first time that the shelves were
located in recesses or niches surrounding the
hall; we have discovered how students or
librarians could reach these shelves, even if
very high above the floor; and where the readers sat; and whence came the proper amount of
light, and so on. The discovery at Timgad has,
in fact, opened new horizons to us and has
enabled us to identify many classic buildings,
which had remained nameless. Who would
have thought, for instance, that the so-called
" Sala dei Filosofi " in Hadrian's villa was
but the library annexed to the Emperor's
residence, where his guests were sure to find
the latest and choicest works of poets and
historians? Who would have thought that the
two hemicycles of Trajan's Forum and the
hall of Agrippa's baths in the *via della Palom-
bella* had the same function? My own personal experience has been wide and successful

in this line of research, and I have been able
to identify the library, belonging to the
baths of Caracalla. In fact, there were two
libraries in that immense establishment, one
for Latin and one for Greek literature, with
spaces for busts, medallions, and effigies of the
leaders in every branch of human learning,
History, Philosophy, Art, Law, Medicine, and
so on.

This discovery deserves a few words of
illustration. While engaged in 1908 in laying
out the Passeggiata archeologica, it became
part of my scheme to reconstruct the formal
garden of Caracalla's Baths, where the fashionable clients were wont to take their constitu-
tional. This garden with its gravel paths,
crossing each other at right angles, and with its
borders of boxwood enclosing the green lawns
and the shrubberies of laurel and myrtle, occupied the whole space, which stretched between the central halls (*frigidarium, tepida-
rium, caldarium*) and the perimetral buildings,
such as reading rooms, lecture rooms and galleries for the exhibition of curiosities and
novelties. The noblest and most sumptuous
apartment, which I happened to bring to
light, was so identical in every detail (although

[ 87 ]

on a much grander scale) with the Municipal
Library discovered by Ballu at Timgad, that
identification became as easy, as it was absolutely sure. The hall, which was built against
the cliff of the smaller Aventine, was protected
by a double wall, with free space for ventila-
tion and for circulation of hot air. There were
the narrow stairs leading up to the higher rows
of shelves, and marble benches for the accom-
modation of students and readers, and many
other essential characteristics with which
Ballu's description of his own discovery has
made us familiar.[33]

Another particular deserves notice. When
Pope Gregory XIII built his magnificent " Cappella Gregoriana " in St. Peter's, he made use
of columns of grey porphyry, unique of their
kind, and for a long time of unknown origin.
Their source, however, has been discovered,
thanks to the recovery of the workshop in
which Pope Gregory's stone-cutters adapted
the shafts to their new destination, and our
finding, there, a great number of shapeless
blocks and fragments of that unique species
of marble. The columns had once ornamented the façade of the ancient Library.
We shall henceforth reckon the good Pope

Buoncompagni among the despoilers of Caracalla's Baths.

As regards private institutions of this nature,
I remember walking one day up the Clivus
Suburanus (via di Santa Lucia in Silice) where
a spacious hall was just being laid bare. I
noticed that the walls were rough and un-
plastered up to a certain height, but beautifully
decorated in stucco work above the seven-foot
line. The decorations consisted of fluted
pilasters enclosing square panels, in the centre
of which were medallions in low relief, two
feet in diameter. As always happens in these
cases, the precious portraits were gone, but
not their frames, on one of which I read,
written in red colour, APOLLONIVS THYAN,
. . . *i.e.* the name of *Apollonius from
Thyana*, which told as plainly the purpose of
the apartment as if the actual bookshelves and
their contents had been found *in situ*. We
know from the description of the library of
St. Isidore at Hispalis that on the frieze of the
*armaria*, containing works of a given subject,
the portraits of the principal authors were
painted, together with epigrams explaining the
contents of the *armaria*.

By a singular misfortune, to be deeply regretted, the two greatest public libraries of Rome, the *bibliotheca Apollinis* and the *bibliotheca Octaviae,* have never been laid bare, although their site and extent are known with absolute precision, and although their exploration could be accomplished with no difficulty whatever, by a small group of workmen and the outlay of a few thousand lire. It may be the perversity of Fate or the perversity of man, — but these libraries are still lying under their shroud of rubbish, awaiting a merciful hand to lift it and to accomplish one of the greatest discoveries of the age. The area of the *bibliotheca Octaviae* is still used for an evil-smelling fish market, and that of the *bibliotheca Apollinis* for a kitchen garden! Both were magnificent structures. The first occupied two wings of the portico surrounding temples of Jupiter and Juno, and was connected with a *schola* or lecture-hall, which was decorated with a set of pictures by Antiphilus and with famous works of statuary, such as the " Cupid with the Thunderbolt," attributed by some to Scopas, by others to Praxiteles. The Cupid had been the property of Phryne, who had willed it to the city of Thespiae. Caligula seized it, in spite of the remonstrances of the

Thespians. Claudius restored it to its legal owners, but Nero took it away for the second time. It perished in the fire of Titus.

On April 13, 1870, I was able to ascertain the fact that some of the artistic treasures of Octavia's libraries still lie buried a few feet below the surface of the ground. I refer to the discovery of an oblong marble pedestal, bearing the signature OPVS TISICRATIS — the " opus " being a work of bronze representing a chariot guided by a woman. The bronze work was lost but it was replaced by a statue of Cornelia, mother of the Gracchi, represented in a sitting posture.

The palace of the Caesars contained many literary treasures; the *Bibliotheca Tiberiana* was set apart for the safe-keeping of State documents. There were, besides, the *Flavian* library in the Forum of Peace, and the *Ulpian* in the Forum of Trajan. The last, the richest and most magnificent of the metropolis, was especially renowned for its set of *libri elephantini* (books with leaves of ivory), which Diocletian removed to his own Baths by the end of the third century.

We are tolerably well acquainted with the sad end of most of the ancient Roman

libraries. Those of Octavia perished in the
fire of Titus, 80 A.D. The one of Tiberius
seems to have shared the same fate in the fire
of Commodus, 191 A.D. The one annexed to
the Temple of Jupiter on the Capitol was
annihilated by a thunderbolt about 275 A.D.
That of Apollo caught fire in the night between the 18th and the 19th of March, 363
A.D., the conflagration being so sudden and so
violent that the Sibylline books alone were
saved out of many thousands of volumes.

Such, then, was the organization of the
" temples of learning " in ancient Rome. Did
the organization perish with the fall of the
Empire, or was its inheritance accepted by the
Church? Did the fathers of the church acknowledge its importance? Can we pretend
that the Vatican library, as reconstructed by
Sixtus IV, represents a direct transmission
from classic times and from the golden age of
Asinius Pollio and Augustus? There is no
doubt about the answer. The church accepted
and continued the Greek and Roman tradition.
That Christian communities, since the Apos-
tolic times, were provided with libraries of
sacred books is proved by many passages in
the *Acta Martyrum,* from the time of Nero to

that of Julian the Apostate. In the *Acts* of
Minucius Felix it is related how the magistrates
of Cirta went to the meeting-house of the Chris-
tians and opened the library to seize the books;
but the shelves were found empty. Other instances have been quoted in my *Ancient
Rome*.[34]

The first building erected in Rome under the
Christian rule, for the study and preservation
of books and documents, was the *Archivum* of
Pope Damasus, who occupied the chair of St.
Peter's between 366 and 384. He selected for
the site of his establishment the barracks or
stables of the Green Charioteers (*Statio Fac-
tionis Prasinae*) and modelled the structure on
the pattern of the typical library at Pergamum, of which that of Apollo on the Palatine
had been a worthy rival. He began by raising a chapel to St. Lawrence in the centre
of the area, which corresponds to the Temple of
Minerva at Pergamum and to the Temple of
Apollo in Rome. The hall of St. Lawrence,
which still exists under a different shape
(Chiesa di San Lorenzo in Damaso), was surrounded by a square portico, into which opened
the rooms or chambers containing the various
apartments for the archives and for the library.

[ 93 ]

Mention of this building is frequently made in the literature of the fourth and fifth centuries, up to the year 501 A.D. The first blow aimed at the institution took place in the seventh century, when the archives of the church were centralized at the Lateran. Finally the building itself, repaired and probably disfigured from time to time, was levelled to the ground in 1486 by Cardinal Raphael Riario, nephew of Sixtus IV. A new church was then built two hundred feet east of the old basilica, and incorporated by Riario in his magnificent Palazzo della Cancelleria. Those who have visited Rome cannot have forgotten the wonderful courtyard of this Palace, the *chef d'oeuvre* of Bramante, resting (as by a miracle of art) on a double tier of slender granite columns. These are the very ones which Pope Damasus carried from the barracks of the Greens to his library, and which Cardinal Riario in 1486 removed from the library to his palace.

Such in brief was the nature and the history of ancient temples of learning in Rome, and similarly in Greece and in the more civilized provinces of the Empire. Can modern institutions be advantageously compared with the ancient ones? I do not hesitate answering in the affirmative. In fact, I believe that such libraries as the Vatican, the British Museum, and the Nazionale are superior to those of the Romans and of the Alexandrians from every point of view, only one excepted. The Roman and the Alexandrian libraries contained masterpieces of literature which, alas! are lost to us forever.

## IX.  POLICE  AND  FIRE
## DEPARTMENTS

THE organization of police in ancient
and modern Rome offers some curious points of identity and compar-
ison.  In the first place there was then, as there
is now, a distinction between ordinary police-
men, detailed to keep peace and order and to
prevent crime within the radius of the Metropolitan district of the city, and detectives or investigating or political agents.  The first were
called *Vigiles,* the others, *Frumentarii* or *Peregrini,* a denomination the origin of which is not
clear.  The *Vigiles* are still alive: it is a municipal body of firemen, called " Pompieri," always
on the alert not only for cases of conflagration,
but also, in the event of earthquakes, of collapse of buildings, of inundations and so on.
The *Frumentarii* and the *Peregrini,* detectives,
spies, criminal investigating agents, have
changed their name *(Guardie Regie),* but not
their duties.  They differ, however, in the style
of their lodgings.  The classic barracks on

the Caelian Hill could almost be compared with a princely residence, with their large courts enclosed by colonnades of precious marble; with temples where they were wont to perform their religious rites, and with secret lodges for such men as were imbued with the mysterious worship of Mithras and Cybele. One of these mysterious grottoes was discovered in 1567 near the church of la Navicella.

The total number of " keepers of order," including the inspectors of public markets (*Urbani*) and of urban and suburban traffic, was about nine thousand men. The way we have learned these details is rather interesting.

In January, 1820, two marble pedestals were found near the gate of the Villa Celimontana (Mattei) in their original position, viz. in the vestibule of the barracks of the fifth Battalion (*Statio Cohortis V Vigilum*). The first pedestal bore no dedicatory inscription, therefore no date. The second (and the statue upon it) had been offered to Caracalla in the year 210 by the Prefect of Police, the Adjutant General, the Colonel of the fifth Battalion, the Captains of the seven companies, the four physicians and surgeons attached to the barracks, etc.

It appears from this document that in the year 205, which is the approximate date of the first pedestal, the battalion numbered 113 officers and 930 men. In the year 210 the number of the former had decreased to 109, while the number of the latter had increased to 1,113. Taking as the average strength of a battalion 1,033 men all told, the whole police force of the Metropolis must have numbered 7,231 men. Comparing these figures with the total of the population, it is evident that the proportion between the number of citizens and the number of police in Rome is about the same to-day as it was under the Empire.

It is also a remarkable coincidence that the Headquarters, the Scotland Yard of the Roman Police, should occupy to-day the same site, almost the same building as of old. As a matter of fact, the building, now annexed to the Church of San Marcello, has only changed its old name of *Statio Cohortis I Vigilum* into the prosaic one of *Questura Centrale*. The remains of the *Statio* were found in 1644, at the time of Pope Barberini, in the foundations of the palazzo Muti-Savorelli, now Balestra. Luke Holstenius, an eye witness, speaks of large halls with columns, pedestals, marble incrustations, mosaic pavements, waiting rooms and offices with marble seats around the walls: of eight statues of gods and emperors, and of an exquisite bas-relief representing Perseus and Andromeda (now in the casino of the Villa Doria Pamphili). Fancy the office of Inspector Brown in Scotland Yard, with Perseus and Andromeda, chiselled by a Greek master, staring down upon his desk! Bartoli [35] speaks of two more bas-reliefs, broken to pieces and buried again by the Cavaliere Muti in the foundation of his palace, and of a colossal statue which shared the same fate by order of the monks of San Marcello. *18277*

I have discovered, or witnessed the discovery of the *excubitorium* or corps-de-garde of the seventh battalion near the Church of San Crisogono in the Trastevere, and of the beautiful quarters of the Police at Ostia. The site of the fourth battalion near the Church of San Saba was revealed by the discovery of a pedestal, dating from 205 A.D., and inscribed with the following remarkable statement: " Severus and Caracalla Emperors, to Junius Rufinus prefect of the Vigiles, greetings. You are hereby authorized to punish with the rod, or with the cat-o'-nine-tails (*fustibus vel fla-*

*gellis*) the janitor or any of the inhabitants of
a house in which fire has broken out through
negligence.  In case the fire should be caused
not by negligence but by crime, you must hand
over the incendiaries to the Prefect of the city.
Remember also that one of your duties is to
track runaway slaves and to return them to
their masters."

During performances in the Coliseum, the
air was kept cool and fragrant by the sprays
of many fountains and refreshed by pleasant
aromas.  The arena, or floor of the amphitheatre, was made to assume various aspects according to the place of origin and the variety
of the wild animals to be hunted to death.  At
one moment the arena would be shaded by
the palms and tamarisks of the sandy wastes,
at another it would be broken into the rocks
and icy caverns of Thrace; and when amphib-
ious animals and other monsters of the deep
were made to appear, what had just before
appeared as a garden or a forest was suddenly
changed into a pond surrounded by lotus
plants and other Nubian reeds.  The nets
which protected the spectators from the on-
rush of wild beasts were occasionally gilded,
and the aisles or corridors leading to the seats

were studded with cut glass in imitation of jewels.

The amphitheatre erected by Scribonius Curio in 46 B.C., was essentially a double theatre, the two semicircular elements of which revolved on pivots and rollers, so that they could be brought face to face and closed to form one, unique, round building, without having the spectators leave their seats.

One may readily imagine the difficulty of the task imposed upon the Roman police to keep such crowds in order and to marshal the various classes of citizens to the seats or spaces allotted to each of them. To facilitate this duty the Coliseum was provided with 64 exits, and the staircases were constructed with such skill that people ascending or descending them could not possibly interfere with one another.

At the time of its great prosperity — *viz.*, in the second half of the second century of our era — Rome boasted of three theatres, three amphitheatres, three circuses, one Odeum, and one Stadium, besides other places of less importance, created for various kinds of spectacles, to be found, *e.g.*, in the villas and parks of Domitian, Gallienus, Maxentius, and even in those of private citizens, like the Quintilii on the Appian Way, and the Septimii on the via Tusculana. According to the official almanac of the Empire, of which we possess two editions, the first (*Notitia*) dating from 334 A.D., the second (*Curiosum*) dating from about 357 A.D., these buildings were capable of accommodating the following number of spectators:

| | |
|---|---:|
| The Flavian Amphitheatre......... | 87,000 |
| The Theatre of Balbus........... | 71,600 |
| The Theatre of Marcellus......... | 20,500 |
| The Odeum of Domitian......... | 11,600 |
| The Stadium of Alexander Severus.. | 30,088 |
| The Circus Maximus............. | 385,000 |
| TOTAL......... | 605,788 |

Perhaps there is exaggeration in these figures; in fact, Huelsen has shown by careful computation that scarcely 140,000 persons could find room in the Circus Maximus. Whether he be right or wrong, the fact remains that, compared with such enormous capacities, the largest of our modern theatres, auditoriums, aquariums, and concert halls sinks into insignificance.

A question to which catastrophes of even the

present time lend special interest is whether the Roman public buildings were absolutely fire-proof. And, in case they were not, what pre-cautions were taken by the police to keep under control, to protect, and to save from annihilation those vast crowds, in case of a sudden outburst of fire? As to the first ques-tion, I do not hesitate to say that ancient the-atres and amphitheatres were not fireproof. When we find ourselves in the presence of their mighty ruins; when we behold those great masses of marble and stone, that seem to defy eternity itself, we feel ready to scorn the idea that fire could destroy or damage them; yet, such things came to pass, however difficult we find it to explain the occurrences. On August 23, 217 A.D., Macrinus being Emperor, the Flavian Amphitheatre was struck by lightning and set ablaze. The 49 companies of firemen, helped by detachments of marines from the naval stations of Misenum and Ravenna, who happened to be quartered in Rome at that time, did not gain control of the flames, in spite of the use of a heavy water spout, until the stone and marble work of the upper tiers had suffered great damage; so great, indeed, that the amphi-theatre was altogether abandoned for the time being, and the celebration of the gladitorial and hunting games was transferred to the Circus. It took six full years to rebuild the damaged sections. The restorations made by Heliogabalus and Alexander Severus can be seen to the present day from the upper balcony: a patchwork of stones of every description, of trunks of columns, of pieces of entablatures, lintels and architraves recovered from the sections injured by the conflagration, or taken from other buildings.

The Theatre of Marcellus, the remains of which form the mound known as " Monte Savello " (from the patrician family of that name once entrenched within its arcades), was burnt twice — once in the fire of Nero, July, 65, and again in the fire of Titus in 81. Worse even, was the fate of the Theatre of Pompey the Great, which was gutted not less than four times in the space of 337 years. As regards the Circus Maximus, we know that the fire of Nero, which destroyed half the city, originated among the inflammable materials accumulated under the lower arcades of the building. The damage was so great that in order to save time and money, and to avoid the tedious work of quarrying millions of cubic feet of stone, the Naumachia of Domitian was demolished and its stone and marble blocks were used for the reconstruction of the Circus.

We are bound, then, to acknowledge that Roman spectacular buildings were not safe from fire. But how can we reconcile this with the fact that they were apparently but a mass of solid masonry and solid stone?

Let us answer first as regards the Coliseum. We know from the Records of the Arval Brotherhood [36] that the eleven highest rows of seats were of wood, their aggregate length being 18,480 feet, and their framework strong enough to support a crowd of 13,860 spectators. We may compute, then, the approximate quantity of timber accumulated near the top of the building at one hundred to one hundred and fifty thousand cubic feet, a prodigious mass of fuel, made more inflammable by the fierce heat of a Roman summer (the fire occurred Aug. 23, 217 A.D.). As regards the theatres, fire frequently broke out on the stage and destroyed it, but did very little damage to the rest of the building. We know that in the year 283 the stage of the Pompeian theatre was encumbered with all kinds of inflammable tinsel for the performance of pantomimes. The Romans were exceedingly fond of this kind of show, and the "mise en scène" of popular pieces was such an elaborate display of ingenuity, magnificence, and attention to details, that, in comparison, all our present attempts of the same sort sink into insignificance. The few details on the subject which have reached us sound imaginary. On one occasion King Tiridates of Armenia was invited by Nero to watch the performance from the Imperial box; the whole theatre of Pompey, — stage, seats, boxes, balconies, — was gilded for this occasion. The awnings spread over the *cavea,* to protect the spectators from the sun, were made of Tyrian purple gauze which was dotted with stars of gold and bore the image of Nero woven or embroidered in the centre of it under the attributes of the Sun guiding his *quadriga.*

A splendid monumental record of the facts discussed in this chapter was discovered in 1893 near the church of S. Andrea del Noviziato in the foundations of the new "Ministero della casa Reale." This monumental record, unknown except to a few specialists to whom permission of viewing it has been granted by the Minister, refers to the fire of Nero, which destroyed half the city in the month of July,

65 A.D. The citizens, overwhelmed by the greatness of the calamity, made a vow for the annual celebration of expiation ceremonies, *viz.*, sacrifices on altars raised for the purpose in each of the fourteen regions of the Metropolis. The vow was, however, forgotten, until Domitian claimed its fulfillment some twenty or twenty-five years later. The altar discovered on the Quirinal is particularly interesting on account of its proximity to Domitian's paternal house, which stood at the corner of the two streets named respectively *Alta Semita* and *ad Malum Punicum*.

The altar, about twenty feet long and nine wide, stood in the middle of a paved area, lined with stone *cippi,* which were placed at intervals of eight feet and bore the following inscription: " This sacred area, marked with stone cippi and enclosed with a hedge, as well as the altar which stands in the middle of it, were dedicated by the Emperor Domitian in consequence of an unfulfilled vow made by the citizens at the time of the fire of Nero." The dedication is made subject to the following rule: that no one shall be allowed to loiter, trade, build, or plant trees or shrubs within the line of terminal stones; that on August

twenty-third of each year, the day of the
Vulcanalia, the magistrate presiding over each
region shall sacrifice on the altar a red calf
and a pig; that he shall address to the gods
the following prayer (the text is missing).
This inscription was known at the end of
the fifteenth century and read again in 1644,
when Pope Barberini was laying the foundations of the church of S. Andrea.

# X.  SUMMER  RESORTS

AT  the  time  of  its  greatest  prosperity
it  was  impossible  to  determine  how
far  the  Metropolitan  district  extended  into  the  Campagna,  because  the  zones
or  belts  of  the  *continentia  aedificia*  (houses
adjoining  each  other),  of  the  *expatiantia  tecta*
(houses  standing  on  their  own  ground),  and  of
the  *extrema  tectorum*  (scattered  habitations,
surrounded  by  gardens  or  small  farms)  melted
into  each  other  without  any  definite  boundary
line.   We  may  take  as  indicating  the  possible
extent  of  the  suburbs  the  third  milestone  outside  the  Servian  walls.   The  Metropolitan  district  therefore  measured  approximately  seven
miles  on  its  greater  diameter,  six  on  the  lesser,
and  these,  strange  to  say,  are  the  exact  limits
marked  for  the  extension  of  modern  Rome
during  the  next  twenty  years.   We  must  not
suppose,  however,  that  life,  bustle,  traffic  and
cultivation  stopped  altogether  at  the  third  milestone  outside  the  gates,  as  was  the  case  until
a  few  years  ago.   There  was  not  a  stretch  of

desert land separating Rome from the hill-
towns, from the seashore, and from the volcanic
lakes of Albano, Nemi, Bracciano, Vico, etc.
It was like a gigantic park, dotted with
patrician villas, rising in steps and terraces
from the foot of the hills to the platform
above, each terrace being supported by huge
walls, ornamented with niches, *nymphaea,* and
waterfalls. The millionaires of the end of the
Republic, and, on a much larger scale, those
of Imperial times, owned not one but several
villas, planned and built in accordance with
their designation as winter, spring, and summer
residences. The two ill-fated brothers, the
Quintilii, owned a winter seat five miles from
Rome on the Appian way (now called Santa
Maria Nuova), and another on the slopes of
Tusculum (now called Mondragone), as a summer resort. The Valerii, likewise, owned a line
of villas beginning at the second milestone of
the via Latina, and ending near Castrimenium
(Marino). The same luxury of owning two,
or even three, country seats is known to have
prevailed in the Servilian, the Flavian, the
Claudian, and other families of the old
aristocracy.

There is no denying that the sunny slopes

of Tusculum, Alba, Tibur, and Praeneste
offered admirable sites for the erection of villas
and cottages: but, owing to their proximity
to Rome, and to their insufficient altitude
above the sea, these sites did not give the care-
worn citizens sufficient change of air. Why,
then, did Roman summer residences crowd in
such numbers on the boundary line of the Campagna, in which the germs of malaria were
always lurking, when their owners could choose
more attractive and healthier sites on the Campanian and Tyrrhenian seaboard, on the
Ligurian Riviera, on the Italian and Helvetian
lakes, and among the watering places of Savoy,
the Pyrenees and the Rhine? The answer is
easily given. Traveling in ancient times was
so uncomfortable and so dangerous, and the
hotel accommodations so crude, that private
families, or individuals, shrank from undertaking long and tedious journeys, unless im-
pelled by duty, or bent upon an official mission.
Accustomed as we are to rush across the Alps
in a transcontinental express, we hardly realize
what it meant for ancient travelers to cross
from Clavenna (Chiavenna) to the Curia
Rhaetorum (Chur), or from Augusta Praetoria
(Aosta) to Octodurus (Martigny) by the

Great St. Bernard Pass (Jugum Poeninum). This last pass is the best known of all, on account of recent discoveries made on the Italian as well as on the Swiss side. The road, on leaving Aosta by the north gate, ascended to Endracinum (St. Remy) and to the *jugum* or top of the pass. It was lined at short intervals with "*case cantoniere*" or help stations, one of which has been found at the *Cantine de Fontintes*, a little below the summit on the Italian side. The twenty-fourth milestone is still standing at Bourg St. Pierre, the mileage being reckoned from Aosta to Martigny. The Roman hospice (*mansio in summo Poenino*) stood a quarter of a mile to the south of the modern one, and comprised a temple to the God of the Mountain; a hospice for weary travelers; stables and watering troughs, and storehouses for fuel and provisions. The *mansio* or hospice was a stone structure, with hypocausts and flues for the warming of the guest rooms and the refectory, and with projecting eaves in the old Swiss style, to allow the travelers to dismount under shelter.

As regards the Montgenèvre, the most popular of Alpine passes, a comparison between the old and the present time-tables proves that the mail-coach service between Italy and Gallia Narbonensis, via the valleys of the Dora and the Durance, has remained absolutely the same, and was divided into the same number of relays until the present day, when it was superseded by railway traffic.

The Romans did not care for lakes. Only one villa is to be found on the shores of Lago Bracciano, the *Pausilypon* of Mettia Hedonea, so named because its position on the hill of San Liberato reminded owner and guests of the beautiful promontory between Naples and Puteoli. The same remark holds good for the great lakes of the north, Verbanus (Maggiore), Larius (Como), Benacus (Garda), Sebinus (Iseo), Ceresius (Lugano), etc. If we except the ruins of a villa at Sermione, on the Lago di Garda, attributed to Catullus, and certain reminiscences of Pliny's villa near Torno, on Lake Como, no other evidence exists to show that the Romans appreciated the lake district of Gallia Cisalpina.

As regards height above sea level, our forefathers did not care for the extremes in which we indulge in these days of funicular and cable railways: the altitude of their summer places

[ 113 ]

ranged only between one and three thousand feet. The three highest Roman villas known to me are Trajan's at the Passo dell'Arcinazzo (2,755 ft.), the Anician on the Vulturella (2,772 ft.), and a third, probably of the Antistian family, near Rocca di Papa (2,310 ft.).

A few words may be added in regard to the postal service and its organization. I have already observed that traveling was not a pleasant experience in ancient times; *i.e.*, for the public in general. Government officials, however, generals, ambassadors, magistrates, governors of provinces, members of the Imperial family, courtiers, and patricians had a much better chance, thanks to the skill displayed by the Romans in overcoming the difficulties offered by the barriers of snow, ice and rock, which separated their country from the rest of the world. The Alpine and pre-Alpine roads which they cut across the Maritime, the Poenine, the Carnian, and the Istrian Alps are a miracle of engineering, being still in a workmanlike condition, and still answering their purpose to perfection. Unfortunately they made easier for the barbaric hosts of the fourth and fifth centuries (and for their modern descendants and representatives) the invasion of the rich Italian plains, which have excited the greed of less privileged nations since the dawn of historical ages.

It is true that a powerful military organization had been established all along the frontier to check the advance of the enemy, and many fortresses and watchtowers and signal stations were erected to strengthen the efficiency of natural obstacles; but, strategically speaking, the position of the defenders was, as a rule, inferior to that of the invaders. During the last European war, the defensive and the offensive task of protecting Italy, which fell to the lot of the Italian Army in 1914, was but a repetition of past experiences. It was not the first time that the Isonzo and the Piave ran red with streams of human blood; it was not the first attempt of Huns and their allies to crush the Latin races and to annex the most beautiful and fertile country in Europe! I published in 1916 a Memoir, apropos of these events, under the title *La difesa del confine Veneto-Istriano sotto l'impero Romano*,[37] in which the points of comparison between ancient and modern warfare along the northeastern

frontier of the Peninsula are so many and so
striking that the reader wonders whether I am
speaking of past events or of events of which
we have just been the witnesses. Were it
possible for me to enter into details, without
trespassing on the scheme of proportion between the various chapters of this booklet, I
should mention first, the innermost line of
defence constituted by the entrenched Camp
Verona-Mantua-Cremona-Concordia, with its
four arsenals and its four contingents of
militarized workmen; next, the network of Alpine roads connecting the base line with the
outposts, at the foot and at the head of the
passes of Pontebba, Monte Croce, and Predil;
the telegraphic stations operating with smoke
signals by day and with bonfires by night, of
which stations not less than twelve have been
described in the valleys of the Isonzo and the
Tagliamento; last of all, the organization of
medical help in connection with camp-hospitals
(*valetudinaria*), with their staff of trained
assistants, and with the *veterinaria* or stations for the care of horses and mules. And
as if such a network of defences were not sufficient to insure the safety of the Veneto-Istrian
boundary line, a wall seventy miles long was

raised from Fiume to Vippach, and another of equal strength between Longatico (Unterloetsch) and Catalanenberg (Castrum Catalanum). To conclude this digression, the strategical point, near or at which the fate of the peninsula has been so many times at stake, is to be found at the same Pons Sontii (Isonzo bridge, fourteen miles from Aquileia, between Gradisca and Gorizia) which has seen so much bloodshed during the late war. It was crossed by Theodoric a few days before defeating Odoacer, and by Theodosius after defeating Eugenius. The same unlucky bridge was taken advantage of by the barbarians of Alaric and Vitiges, by the ferocious Longobards (the worst scourge that ever crossed the Alps), and even by the Moslems of the fourteenth century. Not without reason Claudianus the poet sang at the time of Honorius: *Alpinæ rubuere nives et Sontius amnis mutatis fumavit aquis!*

It may interest the reader to know that there were guide books and time-tables for the convenience of travelers, with a short account of the various roads and of their halting places and caravansaries. The title of these venerable Bradshaws was οἱ Σταθμοί in the East,

*Itineraria* in the West. A fragment of one of
these time-tables has been found engraved on
a marble slab, a detail tending to prove that
at the central post and parcel Bureau in Rome,
officers, magistrates, and travelers in general
could obtain official information concerning
the journey they were undertaking, even if to
the remotest provinces of the Empire. The
fragment in question describes the journey, or
part of the journey, from Cilicia to Cappado-
cia *via* Mopsucrene, the Cilician gates or Hot
Springs, to Tyana, Andabalis, etc., and adds
that the journey could be accomplished in seven
days. At all events, there was no necessity
in Rome of crowding public bureaus in quest
of information, as the *Milliarium Aureum*
in the most conspicuous site of the Forum was
easily accessible. It was erected by Augustus in
29 B.C., in the shape of a column covered with
gilt bronze, as a record of the survey of the
whole Roman Empire, on which he and Agrippa
had been engaged for many years. On it were
engraved the distances from the gates of Rome
to the postal stations on each of the main
roads which radiated from the Metropolis.
The remains of its exquisite marble base were
discovered in 1849 near the Rostra.

In the month of January, 1852, an ancient well was discovered on the farm of Vicarello adjoining the Lago Bracciano, where the classic springs of the *Aquae Apollinares* are still sought by crowds of patients on account of their healing power. The well was nearly choked by successive layers of votive objects, the uppermost of which contained Imperial gold, silver and brass coins, followed by layers of Republican silver and brass pennies, of *aes grave signatum,* of *aes rude,* of nuggets of pure copper, of prehistoric objects in bronze, and of flint implements. It was at this juncture that the workmen, who thus far had succeeded in keeping secret their discovery, announced it to the owners of Vicarello, who, by a lucky chance, happened to be represented by the great archaeologist and numismatist, the Jesuit Father Giuseppe Marchi.[38]   The most valuable objects saved from dispersion were three silver goblets, shaped like the " golden milestone " of the Forum, on the surface of which the itinerary from Cadiz to Rome was engraved. Why from Cadiz to Rome? I believe the explanation is this. Travelers, bound from any distant provincial town to the capital, provided themselves with such cups or goblets

which answered the double purpose of a drinking cup and of a time-table; and, after using
it at a given thermal establishment, they would
offer it to the local deity in token of gratitude
for their recovery. A curious fact has been
noted by Mommsen, that although the mileage from station to station varies occasionally
on the first and third goblets (probably by
fault of the engraver), yet the total is the
same, namely, MDCCCXXXX miles.

We must not suppose that summer resorts
were restricted to the hills of Latium or to the
inlets and islands of Campania. Etruria and
the Etruscan archipelago were also sought by
the patrician land-owners, who were bound to
visit their estates from time to time. We have
evidence that in certain rare cases the choice
of a country seat was determined by a love of
sport. Why should the Domitian family, for
instance, have purchased the two lonely islands
of Igilium and Dianium (Isola del Giglio e
Giannutri) off Cape Argentario, and have lavished a fortune in covering these rocks with
buildings of great magnificence? The Domitii
purchased the islands for the same reason that
has induced our King Victor Emmanuel to

lease Oglasa (Monte Cristo), namely, for sport, — these islands being the favourite haunts of the wild goat. Trajan, likewise, built a shooting lodge on the summit of the Arcinazzo Pass, because the neighbouring mountains teemed with bears. Then, there is Nero's villa at Subiaco, in one of the wildest canyons of the Simbruine range of mountains, in which he built three dams so as to create three Alpine lakes especially suited for trout fishing.

The craze for a thermal cure of any kind was one of the characteristics of the Latin race; no matter if the chosen spring necessitated a long and difficult journey. At St. Moritz, at Baden-Baden (Aquae Aureliae), at Wiesbaden (Fontes Matthiaci), at Bath (Aquae Solis), at Bourbonne (Aquae Bormonis), at Dax (Aquae Tarbellicae), at Vichy (Aquae Calidae), at Bagnères (Vicus Aquensis), at Aix-les-Bains (Aquae Gratianae), at Aqui (Aquae Statyellae), etc., where now gay crowds assemble to be treated for more or less imaginary ailments, the Roman conquerors had long before raised magnificent establishments. These famous Spas were not inferior in comfort or luxury to their modern representatives; artistically and aesthetically they were vastly superior.

Pliny the Elder showed partiality towards two groups of springs, the Phlaegreans, and those at the foot of the Pyrenees. He says the vapour baths at Baiae were so powerful that they could be used for cooking purposes. Sore eyes and opthalmic diseases could be cured at Puteoli and Gabii; women's complaints at the Aquae Passeris; gall stones at Stabiae; wounds and sores at the Aquae Albulae; nervous disorders at Cutiliae. There were besides antilithic springs in Syria near Mount Taurus, in Phrygia near the river Gallus, and in Aethiopia at the Red Springs.

Modern generations must be grateful to the Greeks and the Romans for the splendid example they set in the matter of care for the health and beauty of the body, athletic training, the love of open air life, — in short, for whatever was deemed essential or useful to secure a *mens sana in corpore sano.*

# XI. THE FEEDING OF THE METROPOLIS

IN the ever-recurring conflict between producers, vendors, middlemen, and the purchasing public for the necessities of life in Ancient Rome, we find that as early as 440 B.C., laws were enacted, enforcing official tariffs against the greed of wholesale as well as retail merchants. The first attempts were not successful: they only produced a temporary panic, many suicides among the speculators who tried to " corner " the market, and an increase of prices. Another *calmiere,* issued by Commodus, only increased — according to the Emperor's own words — the prevailing famine. The classic document par excellence on this subject is Diocletian's *Edictum de pretiis rerum venalium,*[39] which caused half the stock to disappear from the markets. Blood was shed; supplies became scantier, and prices even more exorbitant. As soon as peace and an even balance in prices were re-established, and the financial revolution brought to an end, life became normal again of its own accord.

As regards the necessities of life and their distribution, I have gathered from Professor Leon Hómo the following information.

Dry bread was never considered a great delicacy, and the ancient Romans were decidedly of this opinion. Public distribution of foodstuffs, which were quite Spartan in their simple character at the beginning, kept increasing as time went on. Presently came the turn of oil, another essential item for the welfare of the citizens. Septimius Severus was the first to distribute African oil, and under him the old grain tickets (*tesserae*) found a new use. Towards the end of the Empire there were in Rome 2,300 places of distribution, while the number of bakeries hardly reached 230.

There is no doubt that the ancients preferred pork to beef and that the Emperor Aurelianus monopolized control of this trade by official daily distributions of pork meat, naturally under police supervision. He did the same for salt, which up to his reign had been most irregularly distributed, from the time of Ancus Marcius, the founder of the *Salinae Ostienses*, to the time of Agrippa, who proclaimed salt to

[ 124 ]

be a state property, and its distribution a state privilege.

Up to the beginning of the third century, the distribution of wine had been completely neglected, because water of a superior quality was abundant in the city. Aurelian conceived a new plan for this branch of public administration. He thought of establishing prisoners of war along the Etruscan Maremma to cultivate vineyards for the benefit of the Roman people. The project, however, was given up on account of the malaria which raged throughout that district.

The Roman government considered not only the sustenance of the citizens; it considered as well the expensive matter of dress. And here also I must mention the name of Aurelian, whose liberal institutions and bounties seemed to know no limit. He furnished his subjects gratuitously with white tunics, with linen shirts for use in Africa and Egypt, and even with those small handkerchiefs which the Romans used to wave, as a sign of applause at public games.

Money has never been a superfluous commodity, but the more fatherly-minded of the emperors provided even for its free distribution at the time of some great public event. Augustus distributed 445 silver pennies per capita, Tiberius 75, Nero 100, Hadrian 1,000, Aurelian 500, and so on. Tickets were also granted to the people, securing free entrance to the theatres, amphitheatres, and circuses, and even for other places of licentious amusement. Thus in many ways, personal identification cards could benefit their possessors.

However, leaving aside absolutely free grants, another method of favouring public economy was the sale of the necessities of life at a fixed reduced price. For instance, certain quantities of grain were drawn from the government hoard and sold at a loss, below the average current price. This was a very old Roman custom, dating from the fifth century B.C. Egypt, Sicily, northern Africa, and even far-away Moesia were plundered to replenish state granaries in Rome, Ostia, and Porto. Later, a specified form of public bread was prepared and sold at public bakeries at a nominal price which, under Arcadius and Honorius, fell to a half penny per pound. The same low tariff was fixed for wine, brought to the Roman wharves by way of the river, and sold under the porticoes of the Temple of the Sun on the

Quirinal hill.  Our experience during the late war, compared with these data, proves that there is " nothing new under the sun," no, not even that invention of dubious utility, the so-called *calmiere* (the fixing of certain prices, with penalties for violation of the law).  The *calmiere* is certainly not a product of our own days.  The first example, concerning the sale of breadstuffs, dates from four centuries and a half before Christ.  When Minucius Augurinus, Prefect of the Annona Urbis, tried to make life easier, by imposing a maximum price on wheat, the people rewarded his good intentions by raising to him a statue near the Porta Trigemina.  I fancy that such a tribute would be neither popular nor acceptable in our age.  At all events, it seems that the edict of Minucius merely stated and recognized the evils of the day, without suggesting any special remedy; it produced, however, many suicides among the *pesci-cani* or profiteers, who had speculated on famine.  Whenever free distributions of food and wine were substituted for free production and trade, at the expense of the State, an artificial condition was created; and economic collapse followed as soon as barbaric invasions and anarchy succeeded the paternalistic rule of Alexander Severus and Aurelian. Political and military disasters were followed by an economic crisis, accompanied by a crisis in production, agricultural and otherwise, and in means of transportation, by stoppage of transmarine supplies, by emigration of peasants and labourers to fortified cities. *Dulcia linquimus arva!* There was also a monetary crisis, because hardly any gold was kept ready to be struck in imperial or colonial mints, and no silver whatever, while copper was seized and cornered by speculators. The only currency left, therefore, was an alloy of lead, zinc and copper, which was made to circulate at a much higher price than its face value. Fortunately Rome did not know at that time the subterfuge of paper money. The result of all these circumstances was a fantastic rising of prices. Of course, the people clamoured for the help of the government, which for a long time endeavoured to avoid responsibility; finally, the Emperor Diocletian was compelled to act; he produced a tolerably good specimen of *calmiere*, from which our modern rulers could learn much, both for better as well as for worse.

Diocletian's tariff, issued in 302 A.D., goes

by the name of *Edictum de pretiis rerum venalium*, of which several more or less mutilated copies have been found in Egypt, at Stratonicea, Lebadia, Megara, Aezanis, Geronthis, Mylasa, and these have been collected by Theodor Mommsen.[40] A comparison of these more or less fragmentary documents, in Greek as well as in Latin, has enabled the editor to reconstruct an almost complete text, which appears in a volume of the great *Corpus Inscriptionum Latinarum*.

The *edictum* mercilessly denounces merchants asking a higher price than the one marked in the official tariff, that is to say profiteers and speculators, and turns them over to the severity of courts and judges as well as to public contempt. At the same time the Emperor declared that even if the sanctions of the law appear to be too severe, it was easy for the people concerned to keep within that law and avoid fines and disgrace. The tariff is divided into four sections, namely, (*a*) foodstuffs, (*b*) *matières premières* such as metals, wood, leather, etc., (*c*) manufactured goods such as utensils, carriages, clothes, shoes, carpets, etc., (*d*) salaries for artisans and professionals.

Did the *edictum* of Diocletian, which neces-

[ 129 ]

sarily refers to most disparate sets of subjects, to salaries as well as shoes, to onions
as well as corsets, to fish as well as university
professors, prove a useful institution?  Did it
bring forth the desired results?  It certainly
caused a quantity of merchandise to disappear;
it caused bloody popular uprisings; it caused
prices to become prohibitive.  But as soon as
the Empire regained peace, and as soon as the
circumstances, which had brought public welfare to such dire straits, underwent a change
for the better, civic life became normal again
of its own accord.  We are at present going
through the same difficulties in consequence
of the Great War; but the voice of our forefathers seems to repeat to us: " Be patient for
a while longer and all will be arranged for the
better."

I have already mentioned this subject in
Chapter VI, quoting well-known instances of
the value of town property in Rome.  Such
values never ceased to rise through the last
centuries of the Republic and under the Empire.  The lack of accomodation was not due
to a sudden influx of immigrants; it had become a permanent evil in Rome as well as in
many provincial towns, caused principally by

the so-called *urbanesimo,* that is to say, the eagerness of the peasantry to quit their farms and fields and become dwellers in big cities. One naturally asks the reason why the ancient Romans did not adopt the simple remedy which is used to-day, of erecting new houses and of extending the new city around the nucleus of the old. There were good reasons to prevent the carrying out of such a plan. In the first place the dwelling quarters were enclosed on both sides of the Tiber by a chain of parks and gardens, which would have to be sacrificed for the sake of raising new quarters and which, besides, were at too great a distance from the centre of business and from the markets. In the second place, the lack of adequate means of communication, considering the small number of cabs and litters, made the scheme impracticable.

Land was expensive, taxes were heavy, fires were frequent, wiping out whole quarters, and speculation was as rampant as it is to-day. Houses were rented and let by floors; floors again were divided into apartments, the apartments into single rooms, each successive holder making good profits out of the proceedings at the expense of the unhappy citizens. This

burning question had finally to be faced by
the government, for the rebellion of tenants
against the rapacity of landlords and house-
holders had led even to riots and to bloodshed.
The authorities first of all forbade the acquisi-
tion of tenement houses for the purpose of
demolishing them and selling the building
materials and building areas, at a profit —
a pernicious habit much practised in our own
time.   As a rule, however, these official
measures had but a slight effect, as we see from
the fact that each emperor felt it his duty to
legislate on the subject, — Claudius, Nero,
Septimius Severus, Alexander Severus, and
others, sometimes in open conflict with established and time-honoured regulations.   Partial demolitions were also forbidden, such as
the removal of columns and marble decorations.
Inspectors were named to watch over signs of
decay and possible danger to the inmates.   In
case the proprietor disregarded the law, the
State itself or any private citizen could occupy
the property and repair or rebuild it for his
own benefit.

Under the Emperor Nero any individual
who owned a fortune of 200,000 sesterces (53,
000 francs), and who employed half his fortune

to build an apartment house, was rewarded with honorary citizenship, a privilege greatly coveted.

The houses of the poor were expensive, without being comfortable, cold in winter, hot in summer, carelessly built, with a scanty supply of light and with poorly equipped sleeping rooms. If rents were in arrears, the poor were frequently expelled, and the arches of the bridges of the Tiber and the colonnades surrounding the temples of the gods often sheltered humble sleepers at night. These complex problems were aggravated by the immense public works by which the Empire altered the plan and the character of the city. The great structures of Caesar, Augustus, Nero, Vespasian, Trajan, Hadrian, Caracalla, Diocletian, and Constantine caused the destruction of whole inhabited quarters without any proviso for the loss. Let one instance suffice for all.

According to Olympiodorus, the Baths of Diocletian could accommodate an army of 3,000 clients. They covered an area of 160,000 square metres, besides providing a swimming-pool of 2,400 square metres. The excavations made in the last forty years within the boundaries of these enormous baths, for

the building of the Railway Station, of the
Grand Hotel, of the Massimi Palace, of the
monumental fountain of the Acqua Marcia, and
for the laying out of a new public garden, have
enabled us to reconstruct within a certain measure the plan of the quarter destroyed by that
Emperor to find room for his *Thermae*. He
had to remove a *schola* or meeting hall of a *Collegium Fortunae Felicis*, a temple built on a
platform of concrete, a portico rebuilt by
Cnaeus Sentius Saturninus, paved streets, and
innumerable walls of private houses.  If, in
addition, we consider that Caracalla's Baths
absorbed a site about as large, not to mention
the Temple of the Sun, the porticoes of the
Campus Martius, etc., all built at the expense
of private dwellings, no wonder that the prob-
lem of housing the population should have
proved almost incapable of solution.  Although
modern Rome is harassed by the same difficulties, I am proud to say that she is overcoming them by going beyond the old three-mile
limit, measured from the Milliarium Aureum.
The next generation will certainly see Rome
extend as far as the Alban and Tusculan hills,
thus — as far as size is concerned — rivalling
the old Queen of the Ancient World.

# XII.  CITY LIFE IN WAR–TIMES

*(A comparison between the conditions of the
Second Punic War and the World War)*

WHILE reading over the decades of
Livy, during the worst days of
Caporetto and the Piave, and especially that part of the account of the Second
Punic War, dealing with the years 218 to 216
B.C., I asked myself over and again whether the
historian was describing events now 2,100 years
old, or whether he had a premonition of those
destined to occur in our own times.  The simili-
tude between the two anxious periods is so sur-
prising, the behaviour of the enemies so similar,
the resistance of the defenders of their native
land so indomitable on both occasions, their
trust in the final victory so firm, that many
events, of which we were witnesses in the last
European war, could be described with the
same words which Livy used in the twenty-
second and twenty-third books.  It is certain
that no modern nation has been led to doubt its

[ 135 ]

destinies, or been driven to such despair as were the Romans during that fatal triennium, long ago. Having lost Saguntum, having uselessly tried to stop the advance of the ninety thousand infantry and twelve thousand cavalry of the invaders, first on the line of the Hiberus, then on those of the Pyrenees, of the Rhone, of the Isère, and of the Mont Genèvre (although the last mentioned were already blocked by heavy snow); having lost the battles of Ticinus and of Trebia; having lost the lands of the Peninsula from which the food supply was drawn, the Romans suffered additional, appalling defeats at Lake Trasimenus and at Cannae, where the question became one of life and death in the most tragic sense of the word. Throughout this long period of desperate fighting never a ray of light shone on the defenders of Italy, never a success, even momentary or partial, strengthened or revived the spirits of the Roman army. The very life of Hannibal seemed to be fatalistically protected by unknown powers. At the storming of Saguntum his thigh was struck to the bone, yet he managed to rise at once as if nothing had happened. Struck again near Piacenza, his wounds were hardly dressed and bandaged when he tried to storm the fortified camp of Victumviae! Afflicted with ophthalmia, caused by the variations of winter and spring temperature, he lost the sight of one eye while crossing the marshes of Val di Chiana. Notwithstanding all these sufferings, this half blind leader, this sorely wounded general, continued to inflict upon the Romans defeat after defeat. In the battle of Trasimenus 15,000 Romans — says Livy — were killed on the field and 10,000 were scattered in flight through Etruria, while only 2,500 Carthaginians were slain in battle. This happened in the autumn of 217 B.C. A few months later, on May 21, 216 B.C., supervened the disaster, or rather the slaughter, at Cannae. The Romans had on the field 80,000 infantry and 6,000 cavalry; the Carthaginians 40,000 infantry and 10,000 cavalry. At the end of the engagement, 70,000 Romans had lost either life or limbs and 10,000 had been made prisoners. No wonder then, that the announcement of such terrible calamities should have created in Rome a feeling of fear and despair, the greater because the people had so much trusted in victory. The people assembled in the Forum, in the hope of receiving later intelligence, but as this was not forthcoming, the crowd was brought almost to open revolution. Those, dissatisfied, kept murmuring to each other: " One of our chief generals has been defeated, the other has found safety in flight; who or what is to prevent the enemy from appearing before our own gates? " Under such alarming conditions, it is easy to imagine what scenes must have happened in Rome and in the allied cities at the announcement of the extermination at Cannae, and subsequently at the recital of the terrorizing cruelties perpetrated by the enemy which, repeated to-day, have called forth the maledictions of the whole world. Let us take an example. Six thousand gallant fighters had succeeded in escaping to an impregnable hill on the shores of lake Trasimenus, where they could have defied the enemy had it not been for the lack of food and drinking water. The next day they were asked by the Carthaginians to surrender and to lay down their arms, with the solemn promise that their lives would be spared. The acceptance of that promise, treated by Hannibal with Punic sense of honour, resulted in the general extermination of the too-confiding refugees. Hannibal, therefore, must be regarded as one of the earliest partisans of the theory that international

treaties are but scraps of paper, to be disregarded at the earliest convenience, and that the
word of an officer and a gentleman is not bind-
ing, when profit is to be gained from its
violation.

With the machine guns fired behind the
backs of poor soldiers, hesitating to be rushed
into sure death (as at Verdun and Ypres), we
may compare the marching orders given by
Hannibal for the crossing of the Chiana bogs,
where the putrid water would reach up to the
breasts of the soldiers. The African and Spanish army corps, accustomed to all hardships of
war, were to proceed as an advance guard; the
Gallic contingents were to follow and push on
at all costs, while Maharbal and his horsemen
had been ordered to kill whoever showed symptoms of exhaustion.

To the war of submarines against food-laden
ships we might compare the action, swift as
lightning, of the African horsemen, who punished with iron and fire the least attempt to
re-furnish with the necessities of life the pop-
ulations which had not given up allegiance to
Rome. The system was the same, as that
adopted by our foes, — to terrorize at all costs!
A superior Punic officer in his barbarian ac-

cent inquired the way to Casilinum of a Campanian peasant; the latter, for misunderstanding the name, was at once condemned to crucifixion.

We have had in the late war instances of wounded soldiers being shot, so as to escape the annoyance of taking care of them. This act of cruelty is described by Livy at the end of chapter 51 of the twenty-second book: "The day after the battle of Cannae, when wounded soldiers had been revived by the cool air of the morning, they were all put to death, while their blood was drunk by other unfortunates."

We have deplored the destruction or even lesser damage done to venerable sanctuaries at Rheims, St. Quentin, Louvain, etc.; but these unnecessary acts of barbarism are not new; they are but a repetition of the example set by the barbarians, whom Livy reproached for damaging the temples of Feronia and Juno Sospita. Nefarious cruelties and depredations of warfare, of which, alas, the Central Empires were guilty, are denounced in the speech which the Consul Cornelius Scipio addressed at Venusia to the ambassadors from Campania: "Choose," he said, "between freedom and in-

dependence, or surrender to an enemy who
never forgets, to an enemy recruited from
tribes who ignore the right and wrong of international honesty, and who speak tongues
more beastly than human." These enemies,
so ferocious by nature, were spurred to new
acts of cruelty by their commander-in-chief,
such as filling the trenches with the bodies of
dead and wounded soldiers and compelling
prisoners to feed, like cannibals, on human
flesh.

Many among us remember from personal
experience the sufferings of the siege of Paris
in 1870–71. After so many years we hear
again of cases of famine, accompanied by utter
disregard of the sufferings of women and chil-
dren. An interesting comparison may be
found in the description left by Livy of the
famine of Casilinum and of the pitiful efforts
made by Sempronius Gracchus to relieve the
horrors of the siege. First, he sent word to the
garrison that he would throw barrels of grain
into the river Volturnus, which would carry
the food supply to the city, as it flowed past the
walls. For three successive nights this pitiful
stratagem was successful, but on the fourth
night, the river being swollen by a heavy storm,

some of the barrels were driven towards the bank occupied by the enemy, and the plan discovered. Gracchus then substituted for the barrels of wheat, loose quantities of nuts which floated with the current and could easily be gathered by means of crates. Poor resources for a garrison of one thousand men! There were savage scenes of the famished, throwing themselves from the top of the ramparts, or labouring to consume the boiled leather of shields, rats and other animals, and all manner of roots. No wonder that despondency spread among the population of central Italy.

One day, when a refugee from Fregellae (Ceprano) had announced the false news of the advance of Hannibal, unchecked even by the destruction of bridges and the burning of pontoons, women with dishevelled hair rushed as if for shelter to the temples of the gods, where they raised their hands towards heaven and implored victory for their men and salvation for themselves. It was at this supreme hour that the destinies of war at last changed, as if by a miracle, in response to the prodigious will-power of the survivors of the disasters of Ticinus, Trebia, Trasimenus and Cannae, and through the supreme abnegation of the people, whose faith in the happy end of the struggle may have vacillated but had never died. So, after many years, we have done and on the glorious battle fields of Vittorio Veneto carried on the proud traditions of our ancestors, saving Italy from what, *deo volente,* may prove to be the last invasion.

## XIII.  THE  TOPOGRAPHY  OF
## ANCIENT  AND  MODERN  ROME

P EOPLE flocking to see Rome from all
parts of the world are undoubtedly im-
pressed by the size and magnificence
of such buildings as the Flavian amphitheatre,
the Baths of Caracalla, those of Diocletian,
the Palace of the Caesars, and such like.  How
much more they would enjoy their peregrina-
tions through the streets of the Eternal City if
they had a better knowledge of what lies con-
cealed under the modern accumulation of rubbish, at depths varying from a few inches to
a maximum of seventy feet.  Rome certainly
was not built on the American plan in squares
and parallelograms, yet it had many streets
which, for directness, length and ease of level,
might have done honour to any modern capital.  The Via del Corso, for instance, the main
artery of the City of the Popes (to which the
names and memory of Paul II and Paul III
who freed its course from mediaeval encroach-
ments will always remain attached), is nothing
else but a modernization and a superelevation

of the Via Flaminia laid out and paved by C. Flaminius Nepos over twenty centuries ago. People loitering in front of the fashionable establishments which line the modern thoroughfare little know that the pavement of the Flaminian Road runs under their feet, at a depth of four to six metres, all the way from its origin at the foot of the Capitol, at the Porta Ratumena, to the third milestone by the Ponte Milvio. Every time I have seen excavations made along the Corso for the purpose of laying drain pipes, or electric cables, or for the distribution of drinkable water, the old pavement of lava blocks has been laid bare. Again, we are proud of our Via del Quirinale (now Venti Settembre), which we think was first opened by Pope Pius IV. It is enough to dig a hole anywhere along its course from the Piazza di Monte Cavallo to the church of Sant'Agnese Fuori le Mura, to reveal its classic predecessor. Even in the heart of the city of the Popes, still involved in mediaeval confusion, we have been able to discover avenues one mile long, and as straight as a dart, as is the case with the Via Recta, which corresponds to the modern Via dell'Acquasanta, delle Coppello, di S. Agostino, and dei Coronari. A third street, name unknown, runs from southeast to northwest under the modern names di Pescheria, del Pianto, dei Giubbonari, and dei Cappellari, making a total of one thousand metres.

It seems that from the time the city was built on the Palatine Hill (an older Rome has just been found on the Monte Mario) to its destruction by the Gauls on the 13th of July, 390 B.C., the Romans dwelt in huts with thatched walls and conical roofs, not unlike those which to the present day give shelter to the shepherds of the Campagna. As long as this system of habitations lasted, families dwelt in a single room level with the ground; but when stones and tiles began to take the place of boughs and boards, the height of buildings increased. Livy describes Tanaquil addressing the people through the windows of the upper part of the house; but she was a lady of royal birth and her style of living was exceptional. These primitive huts, scattered in disorder over the seven Hills, were made accessible by means of rough paths or stairways cut out of the live rock. After the retreat of the invaders no advantage was taken of the almost complete destruction of the city to frame a new and better plan. Each family reconstructed its own dwelling where they chose, with no regard for the simplest rules of hygiene and for a rational system of communication. Livy says that even after the Punic wars had come to a successful issue the city looked *occupatae magis quam divisae similis.*

The first attempt to obviate these evils and to bring disorder into something approaching system and method, was made by the consul Caius Flaminius in 223 B.C. and after, by filling up the marshes of the Prata Flaminia, by creating a Circus in the Campus Martius, and by paving the Via Flaminia. It was a difficult undertaking on account of the constant inundations of the Tiber, which obliged the citizens to move about in canoes; yet, in a short time, the Circus was surrounded by many temples, by the barracks of the charioteers (Stabula IV factionum), and by the shrine of the oracular god, Hercules, " the Great Custodian." A much better and more extensive plan for the improvement of the Campus was adopted in the last century of the Republic, and was the joint work of Pompey the Great and of Julius Caesar. To let the city expand over the Campus Martius Caesar had planned to divert the course of the Tiber along the foot of the Vatican ridge, and to make a Campus of the present *Prati di Castello,* but he was assassinated before he could carry his scheme into execution. Pompey, on the contrary, saw his ideas take shape before 44 B.C., for he built not only the first permanent theatre, with its surrounding porticoes and gardens, but also constructed four temples, some of which are still traceable in the subsoil.

At last came the Golden Age of Augustus. It may truly be said that he found Rome built of bricks, but left it built of marble. Suetonius says of this great man that he was fond of erecting costly structures under the names of his wife, sisters, and nephews, like the Basilica of Gaius and Lucius, the portico of Octavia, and the theatre of Marcellus. He would also urge wealthy friends to follow his example of erecting new buildings or of repairing and beautifying old ones. His call was responded to by L. Marcius Philippus, who restored the temple of Hercules Musagetes (leader of the Muses); by Cornificius, who rebuilt the temple of Diana on the Aventine; by Cornelius Balbus, with his theatre; by Statilius Taurus, with

148 ]

his amphitheatre. Agrippa surpassed all of
them in the number and greatness of his con-
structions. Strabo, the geographer, gives the
following radiant account of the Campus Martius as it appeared in the early part of the reign
of Tiberius: "The old Romans were so bent
upon things and actions of national interest
that they paid little or no attention to the
beauty of their city; but the Romans of the
present day have filled it with many a noble
structure. Pompey, Caesar, Augustus, his son,
his wife, his sisters employed all their energy
and lavished great sums of money toward this
end, so that Rome may truly be proclaimed the
finest city of the Empire." The description of
Agrippa's contributions towards the same purpose is quite astonishing. He chose as the axis
of the new quarter the Via Flaminia which runs
16° 30′ west of the meridian, and filled every
available space with porticoes, enclosure for
athletic sports, artificial lakes, the Pantheon,
the Septa Julia, the Diribitorium, the electoral
buildings, the Admiralty, etc. However, the
Prince who surpassed his predecessors (as well
as successors) for the beauty and magnificence
of his *Piano Regolatore* is Nero, the greatly cal-
umniated Emperor, who, according to tradition,

[ 149 ]

first set fire to the city, thus clearing the ground
for his purpose, then entrusted the care of re-
building it to the two best architects of his
days, Severus and Celer. The account of their
joint work, as given by Tacitus, would do honour to all the Hausmanns and Bagalzettes of
modern times. By holding before our eyes,
at a certain distance, a plan of the mediaeval
city (like Bufalini's), unspoiled by the so-
called modern improvements, we can recognize
here and there sections of Nero's scheme, with
streets crossing each other at right angles, and
with all the essential characteristics of a
modern metropolis.

I take a particular interest in Nero's work
for two reasons: first, because I have seen
with my own eyes a section of the burned
city; secondly because I have found the
grave of Celer, one of the two creators of
the new metropolis and of Nero's *Piano Re-*
*golatore*.

The quarter gutted by the great conflagration
of July, 64, which I have seen and surveyed
and described, is the one lying at the bottom of
the valley between the Caelian and the Palatine, through which the Viale di San Gregorio
now runs. The pre-Neronian city, lying at a

depth of 35 feet, that is to say, 15 feet under the post-Neronian, is in a tolerable state of preservation. The fact that I found great pieces of the pediment of a shrine, in polychrome terracotta, lying *in situ*, shows that the original scheme of carrying the débris of the fire to Ostia, and dumping it in the marshes (as suggested by Nero's technical advisers), was not accepted or executed, but that the rubbish was simply spread on the spot; it also shows that the level of the valley was raised at once by ten or fifteen feet.

As regards the mausoleum of Celer (of whom Tacitus says that he was clever and daring enough to undertake by artificial means works the accomplishment of which nature would have denied) I have found a fragment of its monumental inscription in the garden of Sant' Agnese Fuori le Mura. It is short and to the point: CELERI · NERONIS · AVGVSTI *Liberto Architecto*. The block of marble containing these words was removed from the original mausoleum by Pope Symmachus (498–514), who turned it into a capital for one of the columns of Sant'Agnese.

As if the rational reconstruction of the damaged quarters was not sufficient to place

[ 151 ]

the name of Nero among the most genial creators of garden cities, he linked his name to a park one mile square which was named the DOMUS AUREA, *the Golden House,* on account of its unsurpassed beauty. It is enough to say that it contained waterfalls supplied by an aqueduct 45 miles long; lakes and ponds shaded by ancient trees; with harbours for the imperial galleys; a vestibule with a bronze colossus, one hundred and twenty feet high; porticoes three thousand feet long; farms and vineyards, pastures, fields, and woods teeming with game; zoölogical and botanical gardens; sulphur baths supplied from the springs of the *Aquae Albulae;* sea baths supplied by the Mediterranean; thousands of columns with capitals of Corinthian metal; hundreds of statues removed from Greece and Asia Minor; walls inlaid with gems and mother of pearl; banqueting halls with ivory ceilings from which rare flowers and costly perfumes fell gently on the recumbent guests. More elaborate still was the ceiling of the state dining room. It is described as spherical in shape, carved in ivory to represent the starry heavens, and kept moving by machinery, in imitation of the course of stars and planets. The reason why I am so partial to the memory of this wicked youth is that throughout my long experience, every time I have happened upon his footsteps I have found myself surrounded by *chef d'oeuvres*. In Rome itself we cannot move a step in the archaeological quarters without coming into contact with his name and his work. The same observation must be repeated in connection with his country seats, such as the villa at Subiaco where the so-called Niobid was found, or the villa at Antium, from which the famous *Fanciulla* has come to light. In fact, most of the classical masterpieces (such as the group of the Laocoön) which adorn our museums, come from Nero's possessions, especially from the area of the Golden House.

We must not think, however, that the ancient city, to the study and to the investigation of which we have devoted our lives, dates exclusively from the time of Nero. Enormous fires ravaged his engineering or architectural work, over and over again, as for instance, the fire of Titus, 80 A.D., which considerably damaged the region north of the Capitol, including the portico of Octavia, the Admiralty, the baths of Nero and Agrippa, the Pantheon, and, of course, many public and private buildings

[ 153 ]

of secondary importance. Here we come again to a new *Piano Regolatore*, that of the Emperor Hadrian, made for the reconstruction of the burned districts.

In consequence of these periodical fires and reconstructions, the Rome with which we have to deal is not the Rome of our dreams, the representative of the Golden Age, but a city of the fourth century, far advanced in the path of decadence, joint work of Diocletian and Constantine, of whose clumsy and heavy style of masonry we have such impressive examples as their Baths on the Quirinal, the Basilica Nova, the Sessorian Palace, the Thermae Helenianae, the Senate House, the Heroön Romuli, the Constantinian Basilicas of St. Peter, St. Paul, St. Lawrence, and the Saviour (with the adjoining Patriarchium Lateranense). Just as the damages of the appalling conflagration of Commodus, 191 A.D., were made good by the *Piano Regolatore* of Septimius Severus, so those of the fire of Carinus, 283 A.D., were repaired with the help of the *Piano Regolatore* of Maxentius, Diocletian, and Constantine. And, naturally enough, this being the last (King Theodoric largely *restored* the city; he did not build it *ex novo*), we have no more

[ 154 ]

exclusively classic edifices to gladden our eyes
with the beauty and charm of their outline,
but only awkward imitations of the fourth
and fifth centuries.  There is one exception,
however, of which it might interest my readers
to know.

The ascent of the Sacra Via (Clivus Sacer)
from the Forum to the top of the Velia, where
the triumphal arch of Titus now stands, was
a narrow, irregular, winding road, which had
never been bettered or straightened, perhaps
on account of its connection with the early
days of the Kings.  The task was undertaken
by the Emperor Maxentius who transformed
the lane into the noblest and widest roadway
of the whole capital (with the exception, perhaps, of the *Via Nova* which led from the Sep-
tizonium to the baths of Caracalla — *Pulcher-
rima inter Romanas plateas*).  I discovered
Maxentius' road between March and June,
1878, and found it 23 metres wide from building to building, and twelve and a half metres
wide between the sidewalks.  The reader must
remember that our own Via Nazionale, the
main artery of the third Rome, is but 25 metres
wide!  I am sorry to say that this unique example of a first-class Roman street has, since,

been totally obliterated, without reason or excuse.

After the vain attempt of King Theodoric, of which mention has already been made, Rome soon became a heap of ruins, giving unhealthy shelter to a population which from the million of the Golden Age had dwindled to 21,-000 souls, dying of hunger and malarial fever, while the seat of the Papacy was transferred to the charming banks of the Rhone at Avignon. Rome owes its salvation to the genial Popes of the Renaissance, such as Nicholas V, Martin V, and Sixtus IV, whose initiative was to be magnificently followed in the next century by Paul III and Sixtus V.

The inspiring genius of this revival and the leader of the first improvements in the abject conditions of the city was Baccio Pontelli, to whom we owe the churches of S. Maria del Popolo, S. Pietro in Montorio, S. Maria della Pace, S. Agostino, the Sistine Chapel, the façades of S. Pietro in Vinculis and of the SS. Apostoli, the hospital of S. Spirito, the Palace of the Governo Vecchio, the Palace of the Popes near S. Maria Maggiore, etc.

The aspect of the city was considerably improved by the erection of these buildings.

Early in the fifteenth century the modern spirit, so methodical in all things and so partial to the straight line, began to manifest itself in the cutting of spacious streets through the ruins of past ages and rambling mediaeval habitations. By a Bull, dated March 30, 1485, Martin V revived the classic institutions of the *Aediles* and of the *magistri viarum* (commissioners of streets). Eugene IV straightened and paved several lanes in the Campus Martius; Nicholas V opened the Via di S. Celso; Paul II paved the Corso. Sixtus IV was named " the Great Builder " (gran fabbricatore) on account of the many improvements made under his rule; and Alexander VI carried the Via Alessandrina through the heart of the Borgo Vaticano.

In justice to Pope Sixtus V we must give him praise for designing, three and a half centuries ago, a *Piano Regolatore* which has been accepted and adopted by the living generation in its fundamental lines. It was, and it is in the shape of a wheel, the hub of which is constituted by the group of S. Maria Maggiore, and the spokes, by the straight avenues radiating from that church to the Pincian Hill, to the Quirinal, to the Lateran, to the Gate of S. Lorenzo, to S. Croce in Gerusalemme, etc. This

[ 157 ]

great pontiff was so bent upon seeing his plans carried out that, before the persecution of the Spanish Ambassador, Count Olivarez, could bring him to a premature grave, he knew no obstacles, but destroyed everything which stood in his way, whether great ruins of the classic age or mediaeval churches and monasteries. These wanton acts of destruction possibly account for the change of feeling among the people. The same Municipal Magistrates who had ordered the erection of a statue to him on November 26, 1585, to commemorate the return of peace and plenty, thus announce the death of the Pope to the Town Council on Monday, August 24, 1590: " To-day, our most holy Lord, Sixtus V, has departed this life amidst the rejoicing and mutual congratulations of all classes of citizens."

As far as the latest *Piano Regolatore* is concerned (designed by the well-known engineers Viviani and Saint Just, for the transformation of the city of the Popes into a city of the Kings), what has been gained by its adoption compensates us for what has been lost. Those who complain of the transformation make us think of the miser who mourns the loss of a farthing, while gathering handfuls of gold.

[ 158 ]

Still there is no denying that a great mistake has been made from the beginning by melting the papal and modern cities into one. Had the first been left as it was, as it had been for centuries, had the new city been built on virgin ground outside the (Aurelian) walls, without interfering with existing palaces, churches, villas, and classic remains, we should have gained our end without giving rise to complaints and lamentations. At all events, one truth is beyond dispute: namely, that even in the most complex and difficult matter of city-building and development of city life our debt of gratitude to our predecessors of the ancient classic period must not be forgotten and cannot be overestimated.

# NOTES AND BIBLIOGRAPHY

# NOTES

1. *Curculio,* I. 1. 17.
2. *Hecyra,* III. 2. 22.
3. Rodolfo Lanciani, *Wanderings in the Roman Campagna,* Boston and New York, 1909, p. 6.
4. Frontinus wrote his report to Trajan before 104 A.D., the oldest Ms. of which, discovered by Poggio Bracciolini in the Library of Monte Cassino, has been photographed, page by page, and published by Clemens Herschel, *The Water Supply of the City of Rome,* New York, 1913. It could not have been addressed to a better judge, for Trajan himself had gathered the water and canalized the outlet of the Lacus Sabatinus (the modern lake Bracciano) and brought the water to the highest point within the city limits, by a channel about 38 miles long.
5. For estimates on the amount of water supplied to ancient Rome, cf. Herschel, *op. cit.,* pp. 200–215, and M. H. Morgan, "Water Supply of Ancient Rome," in *Transactions of the American Philological Association,* XXXIII. 30–37 (1902).
6. *Sulla Fognatura della Città di Roma,* Rome, 1889.
7. Other perilous contacts originated in the fact that toilets and kitchen sinks were in direct communication with the infected channels.
8. *Ancient Rome In The Light of Recent Excavations,* Boston and New York, 1888, p. 67.
9. Attendants for private infirmaries are mentioned in the *Corpus Inscriptionum Latinarum,* vol. VI, 4475, 9084, 9085.
10. St. Jerome (Hieronymus).
11. It is a remarkable fact that the site of the ancient temple of Aesculapius on the island in the Tiber is now occupied by the church of S. Bartolomeo and the hospital of S. Giovanni.

12. Cf. H. O. Taylor, *Greek Biology and Medicine*, Boston, 1922, p. 34, in the *Our Debt to Greece and Rome* Series.

13. Collected in vol. VI.² of the *Corpus Inscriptionum Latinarum*.

14. Io. C. Orellius, *Inscriptionum Latinarum Selectarum. . . . Collectio*, Turici, 1828; vol. II, no. 4226.

15. *Op. cit.*, nos. 4228 (vol. II.) and 2983 (vol. I.).

16. R. Gough, "Observations on certain stamps or seals used anciently by oculists," in *Archaeologia*, IX. 227–242 (1789). Sax. Ep. *de veteris medici ocularii gemma* etc. Trajecti ad Mosam 1774.

17. *De Legibus*, II. 24. 60: qua in lege cum esset neve aurum addito, quam humane excipitur altera [lege], ut cui auro dentes iuncti escunt, ast im cum illo sepelirei ureive se fraude esto.

18. Gaetano L. Marini, *Degli Archiatri Pontifici*, 2 vols., Roma, 1784. Vol. II. p. 290.

19. Cf. W. J. D. Croke, "The National Establishments of England, in Mediaeval Rome," in *The Dublin Review*, CXXIII. 94–106, 305–317 (1898); P. J. Blok, "Le antiche memorie dei Frisoni in Roma," in *Bullettino della Commissione Archeologica Comunale di Roma*, XXXIV. 40–60 (1906); A. de Waal, *La schola Francorum*, Rome, 1896.

20. Cf. Antonio de Waal, *I Luoghi Pii sul territorio Vaticano*, Rome, 1886.

21. Eugène Saulnier, *De Capite sacri ordinis S. Spiritus*, Lyons, 1649.

22. John Murray's *Handbook For Travellers — Rome And Its Environs*, edition of 1875, revised by Lanciani, London.

23. Cf. Lanciani, *The Golden Days Of The Renaissance In Rome*, Boston and New York, 1906, p. 310.

24. Henri Thédenat, *Pompéi*, Paris, 1910, p. 27; cf. August Mau, *Pompeii, Its Life and Art*, translated by F. W. Kelsey, London and New York, 1904.

25. In *Notizie degli Scavi di Antichità comunicate alla R. Accademia dei Lincei* (1884) and in *Pagan and Christian*

*Rome,* Boston and New York, 1899, pp. 263–268. The paintings have been reproduced in colour in *Monumenti Inediti, pubblicati dall' Instituto di Corrispondenza Archeologica,* Supplement, 1891.

26. Particulars concerning the growth and transformation of the old Ferriz house into the world-known Farnese Palace, have been collected and published by Navenne, *Les origines du Palais Farnèse à Rome,* 1897, and by myself in volume II of the *Storia degli scavi di Roma,* Rome, 2 vols., 1902–3.

27. Gnoli Domenico, " Descriptio Urbis, o Censimento di Roma avanti il sacco Borbonico," in *Archivio Società Storia Patria,* XVII (1894).

28. The porticoes of Bologna are of an entirely different nature, without any monumental features.

29. The porticoes of Constantine and of Theodosius were the last representatives of the classic tradition.

30. Consult *Forma Urbis Romae,* consilio et auctoritate Regiae Academiae Lyncaeorum edidit Rodulphus Lanciani, Romanus, Milan, 1901.

31. Cf. Lanciani, " L'Itinerario di Einsiedeln e l'ordine di Benedetto Canonico," in *Monumenti Antichi pubblicati per cura della Reale Accademia dei Lincei,* I. 437–452 (1891); H. Jordan, *Topographie der Stadt Rom im Alterthum,* Berlin, 1871–1907; II, pp. 646–663.

32. An exhaustive account of this oldest of Roman inscriptions is given in my *New Tales of Old Rome,* London, 1901, Chapter I.

33. Albert Ballu, *Les Ruines de Timgad,* Paris, 1897; *Guide illustré de Timgad,*[2] Paris, 1910; *Théâtre et forum de Timgad,* Paris, 1902.

34. Lanciani, *Ancient Rome In The Light of Recent Excavations,* Boston and New York, 1888, p. 187.

35. Cf., e.g., A. Bartoli, *Cento vedute di Roma antica,* Firenze, 1911, and P. S. Bartoli, *Admiranda Romanarum antiquitatum ac veteris sculpturae vestigia,* Romae, 1693.

36. G. Henzen, *Acta Fratrum Arvalium,* Berlin, 1874.

37. Cf. E. S. McCartney, *Warfare By Land And Sea,* Boston, 1923, which discusses ancient and modern meth-

ods of warfare; this volume appears in the *Our Debt to Greece and Rome* Series.

38. Consult his mémoire, *Le stipe . . . delle acque Apollinari,* Rome, 1852.

39. Cf. F. F. Abbott, *Roman Politics,* Boston, 1923, p. 154, for further discussion of this Edict and for references; this volume appears in the *Our Debt to Greece and Rome* Series.

40. In *Corpus Inscriptionum Latinarum,* vol. III.², pp. 800 ff.

# BIBLIOGRAPHY

In addition to the books mentioned in the notes, attention should be called to at least the following in this Bibliography.

ALLBUTT, T. C., *Greek Medicine in Rome*. London, 1921.

ALLINSON, A. C. E., *Roads from Rome*. New York, 1913.

ANDERSON, W. J., AND SPIERS, R. P., *The Architecture of Greece and Rome*.[2] London, 1907.

BAUMGARTEN, F., POLAND, F., WAGNER, R., *Die Hellenistisch-Römische Kultur*. Leipzig, 1913.

BERTAUX, É., *Rome*. 3 vols. Paris, 1905.

BOISSIER, G., *Promenades Archéologiques, Rome et Pompéi*.[9] Paris, 1908. English translation by D. H. Fisher, *Archeological Rambles, Rome and Pompeii*. London, 1905.[2]

BOYD, C. E., *Public Libraries and Literary Culture in Ancient Rome, University of Wisconsin Thesis*. Chicago, 1916.

CAGNAT, R., and CHAPOT, V., *Manuel d'Archéologie Romaine*. Paris, 1916.

CRAWFORD, F. M., *Ave Roma Immortalis*. New York, 1898.

DILL, S., *Roman Society from Nero to Marcus Aurelius*. London and New York, 1905.

DILL, S., *Roman Society in the Last Century of the Western Empire*.[2] London and New York, 1906.

DUPOUY, EDMOND, *Médecine et Moeurs de l'Ancienne Rome d'après les Poètes Latins*.[2] Paris, 1892.

FOWLER, W. W., *Social Life at Rome in the Age of Cicero*. New York, 1909. Chapter I.

# BIBLIOGRAPHY

FRANK, T., *An Economic History of Rome.* Baltimore, 1920.

FRANK, T., *A History of Rome.* New York, 1923.

FRANK, T., *Roman Buildings of the Republic.* Rome, 1924.

FRIEDLÄNDER, LUDWIG, *Roman Life and Manners under the Early Empire.* 4 vols. English translation. London and New York, 1907–1913.

FROTHINGHAM, A. L., *Roman Cities in Italy and Dalmatia.* New York, 1910.

FROTHINGHAM, A. L., *Monuments of Christian Rome.* New York, 1908.

HADLEY, H. S., *Rome and the World Today.*[2] N. Y., 1923.

HARE, A. J. C., *Walks in Rome,*[8] 2 vols. New York, 1882.

HAVERFIELD, F. J., *Ancient Town Planning.* Oxford, 1913.

HELBIG, K. F. W., *Guide to the Public Collections of Classical Antiquities in Rome,* (English translation by J. F. and F. Muirhead). 2 vols. Leipzig, 1895–6.

HERSCHEL, C., *The Two Books on the Water Supply of the City of Rome, of Frontinus.* Boston, 1899.

HUELSEN, CH., *The Roman Forum,*[2] English translation by J. B. Carter. New York, 1909.

JONES, H. STUART, *Companion to Roman History.* Oxford, 1912. Chapter on *Architecture.*

LANCIANI, RODOLFO, *The Ruins and Excavations of Ancient Rome.* Boston and New York, 1897.

MERLIN, ALFRED, *L'Aventin dans L'Antiquité.* Paris, 1906.

MIDDLETON, J. H., *The Remains of Ancient Rome.* 2 vols. London, 1892.

PLATNER, S. B., *The Topography and Monuments of Ancient Rome.*[2] Boston, 1911.

PYM, DORA, *Readings from the Literature of Ancient Rome,* in English translations. New York, 1923.

RICHARDSON, E. C., *Biblical Libraries, A Sketch of Library History from 3400 B.C., to A.D., 150.* Princeton, 1914.

RODOCANACHI, E., *Le Capitole Romain, antique et mo-*

*derne.* Paris, 1905. English translation by F. Lawton. New York and London, 1906.

RUGGIERO, E. DE, *Il Foro Romano.* Rome, 1913.

SABIN, F. E., *Classical Associations of Places in Italy.* Boston, 1921.

SANDYS, J. E., (Editor), *A Companion to Latin Studies.*[3] Cambridge, England, 1921. Cf. chapter on *Topography of Rome,* by Thomas Ashby, with bibliography.

SHOWERMAN, GRANT, *Eternal Rome.* New Haven, Conn., 1924.

SMYTH, H. W., (Editor), *Harvard Essays on Classical Subjects.* Boston and New York, 1912. Chapter V, *Some Aspects of an Ancient Roman City,* by M. H. Morgan.

STOBART, J. C., *The Grandeur that was Rome.* London, 1920.

THOMAS, ÉMILE, *Roman Life Under the Caesars.* New York and London, 1899. Chapter II.

THOMAS, ÉMILE, *Rome et l'Empire.* Paris, 1897.

THÉDENAT, HENRI, *Le Forum Romain et les Forums Impériaux.* Paris, 1908.

TUCKER, T. G., *Life in the Roman World of Nero and St. Paul.* London and New York, 1910.

WALTERS, W. B., *The Art of the Romans.* New York and London, 1911.

WISSOWA, G., *Religion und Kultus der Römer.*[2] München, 1912.

Our Debt to Greece and Rome

AUTHORS AND TITLES

# AUTHORS AND TITLES